Faith

DESPITE DOUBT

MICHAEL E. WITTMER

DISCOVERY HOUSE
PUBLISHERS®

Feeding the Soul with the Word of God

Discovery House is affiliated with RBC Ministries,
Grand Rapids, Michigan.

Requests for permission to quote from this book should be directed to:
Permissions Department, Discovery House Publishers, P.O. Box 3566,
Grand Rapids, MI 49501, or contact us by e-mail at
permissionsdept@dhp.org

ISBN 978-1-57293-795-6

Printed in the United States of America
Second printing in 2014

"Everybody doubts. Christians doubt. Atheists doubt. Scholars doubt; students doubt. Your pastor doubts and you doubt. Michael Wittmer takes this common phenomenon and shows us how our doubts can enrich our faith."

—Haddon Robinson, author and Harold John Ockenga
Distinguished Professor of Preaching,
Gordon-Conwell Theological Seminary

"If you've ever struggled with doubts about God, the Bible, or the reality of your personal faith (and who hasn't?), this book is for you. Michael Wittmer fearlessly addresses these issues head-on, providing careful, honest, and gracious answers that make sense and give the reader a framework for a more confident and grounded faith."

— Larry Osborne, author and pastor,
North Coast Church, Vista, CA

"I know from my own spiritual journey that misunderstanding doubt will trip you up. This is why I am happy to encourage you to read and digest Michael Wittmer's very helpful *Despite Doubt*. He addresses the doubts of the mind and the heart and shows how they can coexist with robust faith. This book will greatly assist the conscientious Christian for whom honest wonderings can feel like unbelief. Let Wittmer lead you through your doubts to authentic belief."

—Steve DeWitt, Senior Pastor, Bethel Church,
Crown Point, IN, and author of
Eyes Wide Open: Enjoying God in Everything

"Rather than rebuke or discourage readers, Michael Wittmer has supplied them with help to realize they have ample reasons to believe the claims of Christ. Written in clear, non-technical terms and a conversational style, this book should dispel the doubts of many and strengthen the faith of those who already believe. It deserves careful attention from all who wrestle with problems of doubt."

—James E. McGoldrick, Professor of Church History, Greenville
Presbyterian Theological Seminary, Taylors, SC

"Mike Wittmer is to systematic theology what Carl Trueman is to historical theology: witty and full of (edifying) verve."

—Andy Naselli, Assistant Professor of
New Testament and Biblical Theology,
Bethlehem College and Seminary,
Minneapolis, MN

"Michael Wittmer brilliantly helped me discover that while there is nothing wrong with doubt, there is everything right with faith. As I read from one chapter to the next, I found myself caught up in the undeniably profound wonders of the fully trustworthy God of the Bible. I 'of little faith' realized my puny faith is okay, yet I will get to watch it grow as I daily experience the powerhouse truths of God's Word."

—Doug Fagerstrom, Senior Vice President,
Converge Worldwide

For Tim, Randy, and Phil,
Faithful brothers who passed on what we have received.

CONTENTS

1. Doubt Away 9

Part 1: Belief in God

2. Skepticism 17
3. Pluralism 23
4. Leap 31
5. Knowledge 39
6. God 45
7. Jesus 53
8. Bible 61
9. Belief 69
10. Quest 77
11. Unbelief 85
12. Disciplines 91
13. Faith 97

Part 2: Following God

14. Trust 105
15. Jump 111
16. Faithfulness 117
17. Promise 125
18. Command 131
19. Call 139
20. Fruit 145
21. Assurance 151
22. Heroes 159
23. Believe 165

Discussion Questions 173
Sources 181
Acknowledgments 189

Chapter 1

DOUBT AWAY

For what is more miserable than uncertainty?
MARTIN LUTHER

I have my doubts. How about you?

I have stood beside a casket and studied the dead man's face, looking for signs that he was alive someplace else. I believed his soul was in heaven, but how could I know for sure?

I have heard scientists cite evidence from fossils or the human genome to assert that no serious person could believe the Bible. Their confidence unnerved me, and I wondered whether they might be right.

I have watched Buddhist parents playing with their children, and I winced when I imagined what they would think about me if they knew what I thought about them. Was I mean to believe this family was in danger of hell if they did not repent of their sin and believe in Jesus? I suddenly understood why many people insist that all religions lead to God. It does make it easier to get along with others.

Doubts sometimes intrude when I'm reading Scripture. Every now and then I close my Bible and sigh, "Did that really happen?" Did Lot's wife turn into a pillar of salt, the Nile River turn into blood, and fire fall from the sky to consume Elijah's sacrifice? Did a virgin give birth to a Son, and did this Son grow up to give sight to the blind and legs to the lame, feed thousands with five loaves and two fish, and rise from the dead? *Really?*

Such questions are occupational hazards for Christians in the twenty-first century. Anyone who is paying attention is bound to have them now and again. If these doubts have crossed your mind—and especially if they camped out for a while, pitching their tent on your tattered faith—then part 1 of this book is for you.

Perhaps you are plagued by another kind of doubt. You have no problem believing in God or the Bible, but you wonder whether you are truly following Him. If the path to life is as narrow as Jesus said, then it might be easy to miss. Jesus warned that many people will lead very religious lives only to hear at the end, "I never knew you. Away from me, you evildoers!" (Matthew 7:23).

This can be terrifying. I attend church, read the Bible, pray, and reach out to those who are worse off than me. But when I read what Jesus demands—"Sell everything you have and give to the poor" (Luke 18:22)—I sometimes wonder whether I am even saved. I hear stories of saints who have sacrificed everything to follow Christ, and I wonder whether my life is too ordinary to be Christian. If I was really born again, wouldn't I be more radical?

I remind myself that salvation comes by faith and not by works. True enough. But how do I know I have faith? "Everyone who calls on the name of the Lord will be saved" (Romans 10:13), but how can I tell that my call is sincere? Jesus might be the Savior of the world, but how can I be sure He has saved *me*?

If you have wondered what God wants from you—and especially if you have shuddered from the terror that you might not be saved—then part 2 is for you.

Christians struggle with both types of doubt. Sometimes we wrestle with the objective doubts expressed in part 1:

Does God exist?

Is Jesus His Son?

Is the Bible His Word?

And sometimes we ponder the subjective questions of part 2:

Am I doing all that Jesus expects from me?

Am I even saved?

How would I know?

My response to both groups of doubt is expressed in the title of this chapter: "Doubt Away." This ambiguous phrase can be taken in one of two ways, and I mean both of them.

First, you should feel free to "doubt away." Doubts are essentially questions, and since asking questions is the only path to finding answers, you should go ahead and doubt. Frederick Buechner explains, "Doubts are the ants in the pants of faith. They keep it awake and moving." Have you sat through a class or sermon on a subject you knew thoroughly? You didn't have any questions about the day's topic, and you struggled to pay attention, let alone learn something. The teacher may have tossed out many important facts, but since they were answers to questions you didn't have, they failed to rouse your imagination.

Every discovery begins with doubt, and the largest doubts lead to the biggest breakthroughs. Job dared to charge God with injustice, "Why have you made me your target?" "Why do you hide your face and consider me your enemy?" (Job 7:20; 13:24). When God finally gave Job his day in court, Job realized that he was the one on trial, and he pled no contest. "Surely I spoke of things I did not understand, things too wonderful for me to know," he said. "Therefore I despise myself and repent in dust and ashes" (Job 42:3, 6).

John the Baptist risked offending Jesus by asking, "Are you the one who was to come, or should we expect someone else?" Jesus did not disparage John for his doubts but used the opportunity to clarify the gospel ministry of the Messiah (Matthew 11:2–6). Though sinless, Jesus himself endured history's most excruciating doubt. On the cross He became so distraught He cried, "My God, my God, why have you forsaken me?" (Matthew 27:46). The answer to that question holds the foundation of our salvation.

You must give yourself permission to doubt because really, what is the alternative? If you stifle your doubts and pretend you don't have any questions, you are stuffing a time bomb in your shorts. It's bound to go off later and at the worst possible time, when the shrapnel from your blowout may wipe out others whose faith looks to you.

When you stop and struggle through your doubts, you inoculate your faith against such tragedies. Most children receive the MMR vaccine, which immunizes them against measles, mumps, and rubella. This shot contains live viruses of all three diseases—not enough to make the children sick but enough to stimulate their bodies' defenses to fight back. An immune system that has successfully practiced on small doses can fend off an entire army of viruses when they come.

I was born before the MMR vaccine was invented, and I remember the itching and chafing from my childhood case of the measles. But I did get my spiritual vaccine. When I was in junior high I climbed an apricot tree in my front yard and pondered the existence of God. My adolescent mind chased the arguments back and forth, and after a period of several months—not lived entirely in the tree—I concluded that I did believe in God. I did not wrestle through all of the arguments I would later encounter, but my small bout with skepticism did inoculate me against more virulent strains. Now it would take an extremely powerful argument to make me reconsider my faith in God, and I doubt it could be done.

But despite its benefits, doubt—especially the bratty kind that stamps its feet and demands your attention—is not necessary for a life of faith. This is the second meaning of this chapter's title, "Doubt Away." Christians are known as "believers," so we are people who need something to believe. We don't doubt for doubt's sake. We ponder our questions, not to feed sugar to our doubts but so we can lull them to sleep. It's a good day when you put a doubt to bed, or at least hear it saying its bedtime prayers. The tiny tyrant is no longer terrorizing your day, and he will soon be sleeping as peacefully as your faith.

Some Christians mistakenly coddle doubt. They wish it wouldn't pester them with nagging questions, but what can you expect from a modern child? Our secular age makes it difficult to believe in Jesus, so perhaps the best we can do is make a virtue out of our doubt. If faith requires risk, then maybe it's a good thing that we don't know for sure. After all, how can we take the leap of faith if we know in advance how our jump will end? And so we conclude that knowledge rather than doubt is the enemy of faith. The less we know, the more space we open for the leap of faith.

But this leap *of* faith is often a leap *from* faith. Faith does not mean acting against our better judgment, jumping into the void and trusting God to take care of us. Christians aren't required to begin each day with shouts of "Geronimo!" Faith means to trust or commit to something, and the wisest believers rely on what they know, not what they don't.

If faith requires knowledge, then the important question is not "What are your doubts?" but "What do you know?" The encouraging surprise of this book is that you may know more than you think—more than enough to believe, more than enough to put your doubts away.

Part 1

BELIEF IN GOD

Chapter 2

SKEPTICISM

Faith is believing what you know isn't true.
MARK TWAIN

Recently I was riding as a passenger in a car. When we stopped for a red light, I looked out my window and noticed that jagged fingers of wood were shredding off a nearby telephone pole. I cringed to think how easily a passing jogger might brush up against the pole and pick up splinters. The menacing shards turned my thoughts to Jesus. How it must have hurt His hands and feet to be nailed with spikes to such rough lumber! I shuddered and tried not to imagine it.

So my thoughts ran in another direction. The solidity of the telephone pole reminded me that the cross was real. A man named Jesus was nailed to a post like that. But then I thought, what if He wasn't? How did I know the gospel stories are true? Or what if He was, but it doesn't change anything? How does the horrific death of a condemned Jew on the other side of the world in a different millennium affect my life today? It is comforting to think that Jesus' death bought me everlasting life, but what if I'm wrong? Then I will simply disappear when I die, like any dog, flower, or fly.

For a moment, it seemed as if a hole in the universe had opened up. I had climbed up and out, and I was looking down on the world from above. I felt that maybe I was seeing the way things really are, for the first time. Then a wave of nausea washed over me, and I snapped out of it. I was surprised by my sudden doubts. I have been a Christian for more than forty years, yet the mere sight of a telephone pole had rattled my faith in less than a minute. How is that possible?

I suspect my doubting daydream says less about the weakness of my faith and more about the strength of skepticism in my world. I live in a secular age, when even committed believers walk a razor's edge between faith and nagging doubt. In his award-winning book, *A Secular Age*, Charles Taylor explains that our secular period is a new development in human history. About two hundred years ago it became markedly more difficult for Europeans and Americans to believe in God. Atheists and agnostics argue that this secular step is a sign of growth. After thousands of years we have finally matured into adults who know too much to believe. Christians counter that this secular stage may turn out to be nothing more than a blip, a phase through which every adolescent must pass. Western society grew strong on its belief in God, and once it works through its doubts it may turn to Him again.

Both sides agree that our time is different. There have always been atheists, such as the ancient Epicureans, but they were outliers. Atheists swam against the tide; they had to work at not believing in God. But now atheism, or at least agnosticism (there may be a God but I can't know Him), seems like our culture's default position. We start from skepticism, and we will only believe in God if we find enough evidence to prove His existence. We still may believe in God, but we must fight our way there. Being a Christian today is hard work. It's possible, but it's also tiring.

This chapter and the next one are not going to solve the problem of believing in God—the rest of Part 1 attempts to do that—but they aim to help us understand our predicament. Why is it so hard to believe today? Why does the Christian faith seem like it's merely one option among many, and often not even the best option? How did we get *here*?

Victims of Our Success

Until recently, Westerners assumed the world was enchanted with the presence of God. Medieval Christians would lift their eyes to heaven, bask in the warmth of the sun on their face, and believe they were feeling God's kind embrace. They often took a rustle of leaves as a sign that God was passing by, and they interpreted near misses of lightning and booming thunder as the expression of God's displeasure.

Martin Luther was sure that the fierce storm that rolled in on him was God's way of telling him to leave law school. He panicked and cried out to St. Anne, pledging to become a monk if she would spare his life. Why St. Anne? She was the patron saint of miners (Luther's dad was a copper miner) and those caught in thunderstorms. So Luther's prayer was a twofer. The storm eventually passed and Luther kept his vow and entered a monastery, which set off a chain of events that changed the course of history.

This week a string of angry tornadoes ripped through a large American city, lifting eighteen-wheeler tractor trailers one hundred feet into the air and twirling them around like toys before hurling them to the ground. The television anchor happily noted there were no fatalities, but he did not thank God or even ask what message God might be sending. He simply broke away to a meteorologist, who explained that this impressive "act of nature" occurred because a spinning upper mass of cold air slammed into a stationary front, which had been unseasonably warmed by record-setting temperatures.

I am not suggesting that God was sending a special message to this city, but I noticed the meteorologist seemed confident that his scientific account had sufficiently explained the tornadoes. He may be surprised to learn that the very science that left God out of the conversation could not have arisen without Him.

It's not a coincidence that modern science sprouted in the West. Eastern religions claim that the physical world is merely an illusion, so there is no point in studying it. Buddhism produces few scientists. But Western Christians learned from Scripture that this world is real and good because God made it. They read that God put us on Earth to govern and develop this world on His behalf (Genesis 2:15). So when we research the mating habits of blue whales, the migratory patterns of red-tailed hawks, and the family squabbles of meerkats, we are obeying the first command God ever gave us, to "Rule over the fish of the sea and the birds of the air and over every living creature that moves on the ground" (Genesis 1:28).

This biblical worldview inspired scientists such as Copernicus, Kepler, Newton, and Galileo to study the universe and expand our mastery over it. They kick-started modern science, which has improved our lives beyond their wildest dreams. Modern science delivered indoor plumbing, smartphones, and medication for high blood pressure, which we need to cope with our smartphones. We have gone to the moon, and back.

But our scientific achievements have cost us spiritually. The more power we gained over nature, the less we thought we needed God. Do you see the irony? We studied nature because God commanded us, but we got so good at it we supposed we could take His place. Who needs God when you can solve your problems on your own?

Initially we kept God around as a security blanket. We became deists who believed there was a God who watched over us, but He lived far away and would not interfere with our lives. God had wound the world like a clock and let it go, to run entirely by the consistent tick-tick-tick of natural law. Learn these laws, and you will unlock the mysteries of the universe. We no longer expected God to miraculously intervene in our world, nor did we think we needed Him to. He created the laws of nature, and we could take it from there.

It's a short step from a distant God to a nonexistent God, and deism soon dissolved into naturalism. This secular worldview believes the universe is all there is. There is no God, no souls, and no afterlife. You live, you die, and then you fade away, never to be seen or heard from again. This is a depressing viewpoint, as even its supporters acknowledge.

People of the Middle Ages believed that humans were the focus of creation. We stood between heaven and earth, the image bearers of God on the planet that was the stationary center of the universe. But as Copernicus, Kepler, and Galileo obeyed God's command to study His world, they discovered that we were not even the center of our own galaxy, for the earth revolved around the sun. They insisted that we were still important, for Scripture said God had placed us here to steward this world on His behalf. But eventually even this belief groaned and gave way beneath an avalanche of scientific discovery.

We felt ourselves growing up, and soon we were too smart to believe a religious book taught to children. We were in charge now, and the more we learned to control nature the less we depended on God until finally we displaced Him altogether. Our rise was also our demise, for there is no value in bearing God's image if God no longer exists. The moment we believed we were gods was the moment we destroyed ourselves.

And so our culture is stuck. We cower before the consequences of not believing in God, yet our grown-up minds demand proof that we know isn't there. We want to believe in God; we just don't think we can.

But wait. Backed against the wall by the ruthless skepticism of science, we reach into our pockets and feel a grenade. It's a foolish idea that probably won't work, but desperate people will try just about anything. Brace yourself, for our problem is about to get a whole lot worse.

Chapter 3

PLURALISM

Do you think I care whether you call me Yahweh,
Jehovah, Allah, Wakantonka, Brahma, Father,
Mother, or even the Void of Nirvana?
PAUL HARVEY

Last chapter explored why we often feel it's hard to believe. This chapter explains how our culture tries to free up space for faith, but only makes matters worse. Fair warning: this chapter contains a fair amount of philosophy. I worked hard to make it easy to understand, though you may want to read slowly to fully grasp each point. If you want to know why our culture makes it difficult to believe that Jesus is the only way to God—and even harder to say so in public—then this chapter is for you.

What could be worse than not knowing whether there is a God? Believing that there is a God who dwells beyond our world, higher than we can imagine, and only that. God must be high above us or He is not God. But He also must break into our world and speak to us or we cannot know anything about Him. And if we can't know God, we have no way to tell which religion is right and which is wrong. Maybe they're all right, each in its own way. So let a thousand flowers bloom, and pick the religion that most resonates with you. Can't find one you like? Then make up your own or go without—just say you're "spiritual but not religious."

And just like that, our secular age gives way to a smorgasbord of spirituality. Modern people demand proof for whatever they believe, and since it's impossible to prove something they can't touch or see, they suppose they must do the honest thing and stop believing in God. Here is one way out: We could say the problem is us. Maybe our small minds are too slow to see God. This sounds like a humble solution to our crisis of faith, but as we'll see, it actually frees us to fill the concept of God with whatever content we like. This is the story of the modern world.

From No God to the Unknown God

Secularism announced its arrival in the philosophy of David Hume, who argued that the existence of evil is a compelling reason to doubt the existence of God. In his *Dialogues Concerning Natural Religion* (1779), Hume noted that if beauty and goodness point toward God, then the insufferable presence of evil should count against Him. Hume joked that perhaps our world was made by a young God who was just starting out. Our world was His first attempt, and He hadn't yet worked out the bugs. Or perhaps it was made by an old God, past His prime—the Brett Favre of gods—who wanted one last go before He retired. Or perhaps this world was made by a divine committee. Committees argue and leave loose ends, and so our world doesn't quite work as it should. Hume concluded that the evidence for God is mixed, and since modern people believe only what they can prove, they have no choice but to give up belief in God. Such skepticism may lead to despair, but at least they are being honest.

Hume's arguments startled another eighteenth-century philosopher, Immanuel Kant. Kant agreed there wasn't enough evidence to prove God's existence, but he knew he had to find a way to believe in God, otherwise life would lose all meaning. So Kant made a daring attempt to rescue belief in God, and two centuries later, the legacy of his "rescue" still lingers.

Kant noted that our lack of evidence for God may say more about us than about Him. Our five senses are good at detecting smells and sounds in the natural world, but they are unable to access anything we can't touch, taste, or see. Why should we expect that our natural senses would find indisputable evidence for a supernatural Spirit? A heavenly being would obviously exist beyond what our earthly minds can perceive. We can't know God because our minds are limited, not because He doesn't exist.

Kant divided the world into two parts. The lower story, what he called the *phenomenal* world, is the *world of knowledge*. We may know whatever phenomenon our five senses perceive. I know an apple pie is baking because I smell it; the robin is hopping in the grass because I see it, and so forth. The upper story, what Kant called the *noumenal* world, is the *world of faith*. This world lies beyond what our minds can know, but not what they may believe. We may not *know* that God exists, for He is not something we can see, hear, or touch, but we are still permitted to *believe* in Him.

But why should we believe in a God we cannot know? Kant was an ethicist, and he gave a practical reason: only belief in God can ground morality. If people did not believe in God, then they would readily harm others without fear of eternal consequences. But if they believed there was a God who would reward or punish their behavior, they just might try to live better. So while Kant conceded that he could not know God, he claimed it was still important to believe in Him.

FROM SKEPTICISM TO FIDEISM

Hume's Skepticism: There is insufficient evidence to prove God, so we cannot know Him.

Kant's Fideism: There is insufficient evidence to disprove God, so we may still believe in Him.

God Has Many Names

Kant's separation of faith and knowledge may have been a desperate attempt to rescue belief in God, but it is a powerfully attractive idea to modern people. First, it not only gives them the security of believing in God, but also in a strange way it makes their belief secure. If people don't know that God exists, then no amount of evidence or argument can make them unknow it. They aren't claiming they *know* God exists, so it's impossible to prove them wrong. They are fideists—people who believe for no good reason—and their belief in God is unassailable, at least to them.

Second, it enables them to winsomely accept the "truth" of other religions. If God is unknowable, then no one has a revelation that tells them what God is like. No one can claim their religion is right and another is wrong. Most religions are equally acceptable ways to God, for they all are merely human attempts to speak about what cannot be known.

In this way Kant's separation of faith and knowledge provides intellectual cover for what many people want to be true. We meet devout followers of other religions online, in restaurants, and at neighborhood block parties, and we'd like to think the afterlife will turn out all right for them. Every aspect of life now comes with an embarrassingly high number of choices—my grocery store carries sixty-six brands and varieties of mustard!—so why wouldn't the same hold true for religion? As a *Newsweek* cover proclaimed, "We are all Hindus now," meaning most Americans believe there are many paths up the mountain to God. A Pew Forum survey found that 65 percent of religiously affiliated Americans—and 47 percent of white evangelicals and 49 percent of black Protestants—agreed that "many religions can lead to eternal life."

Pluralism seems like our patriotic duty after the religious terrorism of 9/11, for anyone who claims they have the only way to God sounds as dangerous and divisive as al-Qaeda. Presidents, columnists, and talk show hosts encourage us to open our minds to the religious views of others. Oprah said that "One of the biggest mistakes humans make is to believe there is only one way. Actually, there are many diverse paths leading to what you call God." When she ended her program's twenty-five year run, Oprah closed her final show by clarifying what she meant by the term "God":

> For all of you who get riled up when I mention God, and want to know which God I am talking about— I'm talking about the same one you're talking about. I'm talking about the Alpha and Omega. The omniscient, the omnipresent, the ultimate consciousness, the source, the force, the all of everything there is, the one and only G-O-D. That's the one I'm talking about.

Like many Americans, Oprah doesn't think it matters what we call God because in the end we're all talking about the same person.

Third, Kant's separation of faith and knowledge empowers people to create their own religion. If God is unknowable, then we are free to fill in the blank with whatever we prefer. Does "Father, Son, and Spirit" sound too masculine to your ears? Then call Him "Mother, Daughter, and Friend." Are you put off by the possibility of hell? Simply delete that part. No one knows what God is like anyhow, so you are free to make Him or Her up as you go. And so our world is full of people who claim to be "spiritual but not religious." They are spiritual because they believe in God, but they are not about to let any religion tell them what they must believe. They are religious tinkerers, dabbling in this religion and that to cobble together a God they can believe in.

It's easy to see how this Do-It-Yourself Religion quickly degenerates into a projection of our individual selves. As we fill in the blank with our personal preferences, everyone's God becomes nothing more than a larger version of their best self. And so we combine the comfort of believing in God with the pleasure of being God. The real God can't tell us what He is like or what He wants us to do, for then we would know something about Him. We enjoy the benefit of believing in God and the freedom to do what we want.

How does this work in practice? As with Kant, Oprah refused to allow the presence of evil to eliminate her belief in God. She praised God for lifting her out of poverty and abuse to host the highest-rated talk show in television history, and she inspired millions of women to own their mistakes and trust God to help them rise through the pain. But just as Kant projected his own preferences upon God (making Him the ground of morality), so Oprah turned God into what she felt she needed—a nonjudgmental therapist who empowers us to reach our personal best.

Like other Do-It-Yourselfers, Oprah created a God that seems to be an extension of herself. She endorsed New Age books such as *The Secret*, which declares that we have the spiritual power to change our world through positive thoughts or "vibrations." Our minds are powerful magnets that attract either health and wealth when we are happy or disease and disaster when we are sad. Oprah promoted Elizabeth Gilbert's memoir, *Eat, Pray, Love*, in which Gilbert confessed to liking everything about Jesus except "that one fixed rule of Christianity" that "Christ is the *only* path to God" (emphasis hers). So Gilbert used the generic name "God" when she prayed, though she said she could just as easily have referred to Him or Her as "Jehovah, Allah, Shiva, Brahma, Vishnu, or Zeus." It ultimately didn't matter, for Gilbert said that the god who answered her prayer was her very own voice.

Do you see why pluralism is even worse than skepticism, and is its logical next step? Modern skepticism swept away belief in the Christian God. But people are going to worship something (Romans 1:18–32), so it wasn't long until they replaced secularism's "no God" with pluralism's "any god will do." Maybe they couldn't know God, but they could still believe in whichever deity they chose. And since their new belief in God rests on faith rather than knowledge, it's difficult to talk them out of it. How can you reason with someone who doesn't claim to have knowledge?

This separation of faith and knowledge is logically impossible. How can you believe in a God who is unknowable? How would you even know that He is unknowable? If you knew that He is unknowable, then He would no longer be unknowable, for you would know *something* about Him.

Besides being untenable, the separation of faith and knowledge is the quickest way to lose your faith. Those who are willing to believe everything are liable to believe anything, and they almost certainly will be wrong. Yet despite the danger in divorcing faith and knowledge, many people still fall for it. Even Christians, as I will explain in the next chapter.

Chapter 4

LEAP

Might as well jump. Jump! Might as well jump.
DAVID LEE ROTH

Elizabeth Gilbert had made it. She had a good job writing for *GQ* magazine that enabled her to buy a home in the Hudson Valley and an apartment in Manhattan, which she shared with her good-enough husband. She was living the dream, until she had trouble getting pregnant. Her barrenness led her to reevaluate her life, and she realized she didn't really want children, or her marriage.

So Gilbert left her husband and hooked up with a younger man. When that relationship began to fail, she quit her job and asked her publisher for a book advance so she could travel the world to find herself. She searched for happiness in the food of Italy, the spirituality of India, and the arms of a Brazilian in Bali. Then she wrote about it in her best-selling memoir, *Eat, Pray, Love*.

Gilbert's troubled marriage inspired her to pray for the first time in her life, but the god who responded sounded a lot like her. When she pleaded, "Please tell me what to do," she said she heard "my own voice, speaking from within my own self. But this was my voice as I had never heard it before." The voice said, "Go back to bed." In a few months her inner voice led her to divorce her husband, find a

31

new lover, and study with an Indian guru, who taught her to begin each morning by meditating on the Sanskrit mantra, "I honor the divinity that resides within me."

Listening to the voice seems to have paid off for Gilbert, as her book became a *New York Times* bestseller and a movie starring Julia Roberts. She became rich. She even married the Brazilian.

And she credits God. She concedes that heeding the voice within her might seem foolish, but she believes that faith in God requires "a mighty jump from the rational over to the unknowable." She explains:

> If faith were rational, it wouldn't be—by definition—
> faith. Faith is belief in what you cannot see or prove
> or touch. Faith is walking face-first and full-speed into
> the dark. If we truly knew all the answers in advance
> as to the meaning of life and the nature of God and the
> destiny of our souls, our belief would not be a leap of
> faith and it would not be a courageous act of humanity;
> it would just be . . . a prudent insurance policy.

Notice how she sharply separates faith from knowledge. She believes faith is "a courageous act" only when it runs "full-speed into the dark," relying upon what it does not know. She is sure she has faith only when her faith is unsure. Faith must be a blind leap or it doesn't count.

Every Christian would reject Gilbert's claim to be God (she writes, "I am divine"), but many seem to agree with her assumption that faith and knowledge do not mix. They suggest that knowledge gets in the way of our faith in God, and perhaps attempting to make a virtue out of our doubts, propose that some measure of ignorance and uncertainty is necessary. They argue that it's a good thing we don't possess certain knowledge of God, for those who are sure they know God find it impossible to believe in Him, freely choose Him, or truly love Him. This view is widespread, but is it right?

Do We Need Doubt to Believe?

Recently I attended a lecture by a popular preacher who insisted that faith is the opposite of knowledge. He illustrated the point by making a fist and asking an audience member if she thought it contained a twenty dollar bill. She said she believed it did, because she had read the same example in his book. After joking that he would have her escorted from the hall for ruining his bit, he said "I will destroy your faith by opening my hand and showing you that it's there. Now that you know I have a twenty dollar bill, you can no longer have faith that I do." He explained, "Faith is required only when we have doubts, when we do not know for sure. When knowledge comes, faith is no more."

Is it true that "when knowledge comes, faith is no more"? If this is correct, then the return of Christ will destroy the faith of His followers, for our faith will now be sight (2 Corinthians 5:7). Jesus would not have told Thomas, "Because you have seen me, you have believed" (John 20:29), but rather "Because you have seen me, you are no longer able to believe." Would Jesus ask, "When the Son of Man comes, will he find faith on the earth?" (Luke 18:8), if He knew His coming would obliterate any faith He found here?

Knowledge actually strengthens faith, for it reduces the hesitancy that comes from uncertainty. Faith means to give ourselves whole-heartedly to the promises of God. Right now this commitment includes a measure of uncertainty because we have not yet received all that God has promised. Jesus' return will remove this uncertainty but not our faith, for we will still need to know and trust the promises of God on the New Earth. It will just be easier, because it will be clearer, when we see Jesus. As Paul says in 1 Corinthians 13:12: "Now we see but a poor reflection as in a mirror; then we shall see face to face. Now I know in part; then I shall know fully, even as I am fully known." Paul declares that our knowledge will increase when we see Jesus; he does not say our faith will take a corresponding hit.

The separation of faith from knowledge is the fast train to crazy town. A pastor preached a sermon on Romans 14:23, "everything that does not come from faith is sin." He declared that we sin whenever we claim to know something about God, for if we have no doubts, then we are not acting in faith. He warned the congregation not to say even that they know God is good or that Jesus is Lord. If they *know* that He is good or that He is Lord, then they cannot *believe* that He is—and if they do not believe these things, they are living in sin. Besides the difficulty of trying not to know what I believe—and the guilt of thinking that I am sinning if I am not successful—I wonder what the pastor would do with Paul's confident confession that "I know whom I have believed" (2 Timothy 1:12)? Is it really a sin to say I know God?

Do We Need Doubt to Choose?

Many Christians assert that doubt is necessary to protect our freedom. They say that God could pick up a celestial bullhorn and thunder, "I am God; serve me or else," but then we would be forced to believe and obey Him. God wants us to love Him freely, so He purposefully keeps us in the dark. He gives us enough evidence to believe in Him, but He does not reveal so much that we are unable to reject Him.

I agree that God never coerces anyone against their will, but I wonder whether He protects our freedom with strategic ambiguity. If undeniable knowledge of God and the consequences of sin compel us to follow Him, then how do we explain the many people in Scripture who possessed both but disobeyed anyway? Consider our very first sin, the original sin that corrupted the human race and supplies the template for every sin. Adam clearly heard the voice of God warning him not to eat the forbidden fruit or he would die, yet he knowingly bit the fruit when it was offered by his wife.

Or consider the main event of the Old Testament. Pharaoh initially refused to allow Israel to leave Egypt because he did not know the Lord or why he should obey Him (Exodus 5:2). "Fair enough," God seemed to say, and He set about to reveal himself by a series of escalating plagues. Pharaoh's magicians copied the Lord's initial miracles, turning a staff into a snake, water into blood, and calling up frogs from the Nile. But they were unable to create gnats from the dust and they conceded, "This is the finger of God" (Exodus 8:19). The Lord's existence and the consequences for disobeying Him became progressively more evident as God punished Egypt with flies, plague, boils, hail, locusts, darkness, and finally the death of their firstborn sons. But though his officials warned him that "Egypt is ruined" (Exodus 10:7), Pharaoh refused to repent before the God who had bested him and instead angrily threatened the life of Moses, His messenger (Exodus 10:28). If clear knowledge of God and the consequences of sin coerce obedience, then Pharaoh would have become a follower of the Lord by plague number three.*

And what about those who were on the right side of this redemption? The Israelites saw God deliver them from Egypt and they sang, "Who among the gods is like you, O LORD? Who is like you—majestic in holiness, awesome in glory, working wonders?" (Exodus 15:11). But before the chapter was out they were grumbling for water and before too long they had completely lost their faith and were left to die in the desert. If unmistakable knowledge of God's existence compels obedience, then the Israelites would not have worshiped a golden calf in the shadow of the mountain that thundered and quaked with the Lord's presence.

The biblical story on sin ends as it began. John's vision of the seven bowls in Revelation echoes the ten plagues of Egypt. God's wrath turns the sea and fresh water into blood, scorches sinners with intense heat and painful sores, and pummels them with hundred-pound hail and a devastating earthquake. The victims of this destruction are not forced to follow God, but though surrounded with the certainty of His existence and the consequences for disobedience, they "cursed the God of heaven because of their pains and their sores, but they refused to repent of what they had done" (Revelation 16:11).

---

* Perceptive readers might wonder if it's fair to use Pharaoh as an example of willful unbelief since Scripture says, "The Lord hardened Pharaoh's heart" (Exodus 9:12). As finite creatures we cannot comprehend how God sovereignly directs human lives without violating their freedom, but Scripture teaches that He does. God hardened Pharaoh's heart, but it's also true that Pharaoh hardened his own heart (Exodus 8:15, 32). Regardless of God's role, He still holds Pharaoh responsible for not responding to the evidence he requested.

We should not be surprised by the biblical record. Consider why we disobey God. Do we sin because we doubt God's existence or because, like the Israelites, we are stubborn, "stiff-necked people" (Exodus 32:9)? If knowledge of God and of hell compel obedience, then those of us who confidently believe in both should never sin. But we do. So it seems that neither of these eliminate the freedom that is essential to faith.

Do We Need Doubt to Love and Be Loved?

Besides faith and free choice, we sometimes hear that uncertainty is necessary for the give-and-take of our personal relationship with God. One author asserts that certainty undermines the freedom and trust that fuel intimacy. We seek certainty among impersonal objects that we wish to control, but when we attempt to gain indubitable knowledge of another person we inevitably disrespect their freedom and suffocate our relationship. Intimacy occurs only when we give each other space and trust them to be faithful when we are not around.

The author explains that he could remove any doubt about his wife's faithfulness by keeping her under twenty-four-hour surveillance, but the knowledge gained by his video camera would demolish the trust and freedom of their relationship. He is right about that, but would their trust be ruined by his certainty or by the sneaky way he acquired it? Would his wife be angry because he knew she was faithful or because he spied on her?

His hypothetical video camera is not the cause of distrust and their broken relationship but rather the symptom of it. Anyone who videotapes his spouse or tails her to the store proves that their marriage is already broken. It is this lack of trust, not certainty, that is the death knell to any relationship. Think about it: if certainty hinders intimacy, a one-night stand between two strangers would comprise a healthier relationship than a couple celebrating their golden anniversary. We may never achieve 100 percent certainty about another person, but the more we approximate this goal, the more we may trust and ultimately love him or her. We only become vulnerable with those we trust will not let us down.

I will say more about this in the next chapter, but before moving on, let's recap the point of this one. While it's popular today, both in the culture and in the church, to say that doubt is necessary for faith, a moment's reflection and several passages of Scripture prove this isn't the case. Doubt is not the fuel of faith. What does faith need to flourish? Turn the page to find out.

Chapter 5

KNOWLEDGE

Faith is not belief without proof,
but trust without reservation.
D. Elton Trueblood

Bob and Sarah Chew decided to downsize into a simpler life, so they sold their home in Los Angeles at the height of the housing market and moved to the mountains of Colorado. They wanted a safe place to stash their cash—a vanilla account that would preserve their principal and earn a steady rate of return—so they gave their life savings to Stanley Chais, a trusted financial advisor who had consistently produced strong returns for Sarah's family for two decades.

Bob was nervous about putting his entire nest egg into one basket, especially a basket he did not understand. His quarterly statements were so vague that he could not tell "what trades were made or how they were made or who made them." He was told that he was invested in "private arbitrage accounts"—whatever that meant—and that the "New York people" who were handling his money had figured out a way to game the system, leveraging their volume, a series of instant trades, and a method called "split-strike conversion" to guarantee fifteen percent annual returns.

Bob did not ask many questions because he felt lucky just to be in the club. His high-yielding fund was secretive and selective—you had to know someone who knew someone to get an account. Bob was thankful to ride the coattails of his in-laws' relationship with Chais, and he suppressed his fears by reminding himself that most retirees would envy his position. Who wouldn't jump at a chance to invest in an exclusive fund that paid well and never lost a dime?

For five years Bob stifled his doubts as his investments doubled. Until Thursday, December 11, 2008, when his phone rang during dinner. Sarah answered and turned white. "You're joking? This is a joke, right?" It wasn't. The caller told her that Chais had been funneling investments to Bernie Madoff, who had just confessed to running the world's largest Ponzi scheme. There were no trades or magical methods that outsmarted the system. Madoff had made up everything. All of his money was gone, including the $1.2 million that Bob and Sarah had invested. They were financially ruined.

Bob was angry at Chais for trusting Madoff, at the Securities and Exchange Commission for not investigating Madoff earlier, and at himself for ignoring what now seemed to be obvious red flags. At least he was in good company. Many of the world's brightest stars, including Steven Spielberg, Elie Wiesel, and Mort Zuckerman, lost millions to Madoff's $50 billion scam.

Madoff's victims learned the hard way that knowledge is necessary for faith. We need to know that the people we rely on are competent and worthy of our trust. This is why we demand references for our mechanics and doctors and ask them to explain their procedures before we sign off. We would not leave our car with a mechanic who said, "I'm not sure why she keeps quitting on you, but I'll change a few parts and see if that helps." We would not sit for a surgeon who said, "This is my first crack at your specific operation, but I have always wanted to try it. If you're game, I'm willing to give it a shot." We would bolt out of the chair if we asked our dentist, "Will this hurt?" and she replied, "I have no idea, let's find out!" And we would not remain on a plane if the loudspeaker announced, "This is your flight attendant. The captain is taking a union-mandated nap, but just before he fell asleep he showed me the lever thingy that flies this plane. Prepare for takeoff."

Faith means to trust, to place all of our weight on someone or something. We can commit to virtually anything, but the smart money puts its trust in what we know. We may get lucky with a blind leap of faith, but our odds dramatically improve when we do our homework and have solid reasons for trusting this financial advisor or that potential mate. Imagine a young lady who responds to a marriage proposal by scrunching her face and saying, "Hmm . . . okay?" The man presses, "What's the matter? Don't you love me?" She rubs her chin and sighs, "I guess so." Only a fool would go through with this wedding, committing his life to a woman who is not completely sold on the idea.

In every area of life we understand that what we don't know can hurt us. The less we know, the more likely we are to get burned. Responsible people kick the tires and ask hard questions before they commit. Except, it seems, when it comes to God. Belief in God is the only area where ignorance is not only permitted but often required.

Why is that? As we learned in the preceding chapters, our secular age assumes that God is unknowable. We have never seen, heard, or touched God, so for all we know He does not exist. But our culture assures us that our ignorance of God opens up space for us to believe in Him. We cannot *know* God, and for that very reason we are able to have *faith* in Him. Best of all, because our faith is not grounded in something as certain as knowledge, we may congratulate ourselves for having the courage to believe. We have so much faith we don't need knowledge! And so we conclude that faith requires a leap.

Believe What You Know

The "leap of faith" is a double-edged metaphor for our trust in God. On the one hand it captures the risk that inevitably accompanies every act of faith. Faith is a lot like jumping out of an airplane, with nothing but our parachute between us and certain destruction. We may hedge our bets by wearing a helmet, but we don't really think that will help much if our parachute fails to open. Just so, we may arrange the details of our lives to soften the blow (finding refuge in family, friends, or career), but we understand that if we trust the wrong God—if our God does not come through for us—then we are goners.

The "leap of faith" also reminds us that belief requires our full commitment. We can't halfway jump out of an airplane (and those who try are bound to pull a muscle). We are either plummeting through the sky or we're not falling at all. In the same way, we cannot halfway commit to whatever is our ultimate God. Faith is like sitting. This everyday act requires us to completely commit to the chair. We may study chairs and write books about them, but if we're ever going to sit we're going to have to put all of our weight on this one. Everyone who is in the act of sitting crosses a line of no return. They transfer their weight downward toward the chair, and if the chair is pulled out at the last second, their momentum will take them to the ground. There is always a risk in attempting to sit in a given chair (especially if you're in a room of junior high boys), and so there is a risk in trusting God.

However, many who use the term "leap of faith" overplay its risk factor. Not content to say that risk *accompanies* faith, they go further to assert that risk is the *essence* of faith. And if risk is what faith is all about, then the surest way to increase our faith is to increase our risk. So they look for ways to make their risks especially risky. They seek risky risks—the riskier the better. And since knowledge decreases risk, they believe their leap of faith must be blind.

But a blind leap is not biblical. Scripture nowhere encourages us to trust what may or may not be true, but always tells us to rely solely on what we know. In the aftermath of the Exodus, "when the Israelites *saw* the great power the LORD displayed against the Egyptians, the people feared the LORD and put their *trust* in him" (Exodus 14:31). Likewise, after spending two days with Jesus, the villagers told the Samaritan woman, "We no longer *believe* just because of what you said; now we have heard for ourselves, and we *know* that this man really is the Savior of the world" (John 4:42). John closes his gospel by saying, "Jesus did many other miraculous signs in the presence of his disciples, which are not recorded in this book. But *these are written that you may believe* that Jesus is the Christ, the Son of God, and that by believing you may have life in his name" (John 20:30–31).

God summarizes the logical order when He tells Israel, "You are my witnesses . . . and my servant whom I have chosen, so that you may *know* and *believe* me and *understand* that I am he" (Isaiah 43:10). Notice that knowledge logically precedes belief, for as Paul rhetorically asks, "How can they believe in the one of whom they have not heard?" (Romans 10:14). And belief yields understanding, for our trust in God enables us to learn by experience what we had previously known only in the abstract. We understand God better because we now belong to His family, and so we are privileged to study Him and His ways from the inside.

St. Anselm captured this order in his famous motto, "Faith Seeking Understanding." Anselm wrote, "I believe so that I may understand," meaning that deeper insights into the character of God begin by believing, and loving, what we already know. Jesus admonished skeptical Jews, "If anyone chooses to do God's will, he will find out whether my teaching comes from God or whether I speak on my own" (John 7:17). Jesus wasn't telling them to start their journey of faith with a blind leap (pick something to believe and see if it works) but to choose to obey the Word they already had. If they trusted what they knew they would gain new knowledge to trust.

A blind leap also is not practical. No one thinks it's a good idea to separate faith and knowledge, except when it comes to belief in God. And they only do it in this case because our secular age has convinced them that knowledge of God is impossible.*

---

* Some readers may wonder whether Soren Kierkegaard's emphasis on "the infinite passion of the individual's inwardness" offers a different reason for a blind leap of faith than the separation of faith and knowledge found in Kant. The answer is no, for at least two reasons. First, Kierkegaard fashioned his leap of faith on the earlier work of Kant. To the extent that Kierkegaard separates faith from knowledge, he is repeating what he learned from Kant. Second, Kierkegaard improves on Kant's notion of faith, and in a way that requires knowledge. Whereas Kant said we can work our way to God, believing in a generic deity because we need Him to ground morality, Kierkegaard argued that we are helpless to believe in the true God, Jesus Christ, unless He reveals himself to us. Kierkegaard's favorite example of faith is Abraham. Though an extreme case, Abraham did not

When people assume they cannot know God, they either fall into despair or attempt to make a virtue out of their predicament. Those who choose the latter suppose they are being courageous for declaring that faith is blind but they're leaping anyway. In reality, and by their own admission, they are merely the blind leading the blind.

We avoid this danger when we follow the biblical emphasis that knowledge is essential for faith. The Reformers taught the vital role of knowledge by explaining that true faith contains three elements: *notitia*, *assensus*, and *fiducia*. Faith begins when we know (*notitia*) the facts about God and His great salvation; it buds when we assent or acknowledge (*assensus*) that these facts are true; and it bursts into bloom when we wholeheartedly trust (*fiducia*) what we know. In this way faith involves the entire person committing intellect, will, and affections to God.

John Calvin was so sure that faith must rest on knowledge that he defined faith as "a firm and certain *knowledge* of God's benevolence toward us" (my emphasis). He wasn't reducing faith to mere head knowledge, for he added that the assent of faith "is more of the heart than of the brain" and that faith must commit to what it knows to count as true faith. Just to be sure, the Heidelberg Catechism improved on Calvin's definition by noting, "True faith is *not only a knowledge* and conviction that everything God reveals in his Word is true; it is also a *hearty trust*" (my emphasis). Faith can't get started without knowledge, but it misfires if we don't give ourselves to what we know.

Here's the point: faith means to trust, commit, or put all of our weight on someone or something. Because faith requires us to go all in, the smart money always trusts what it knows, not what it doesn't. But this begs the question, What do you know? Do you know enough about God to believe in Him? We examine this question next.

---

blindly sacrifice Isaac but wholeheartedly relied on the promise and command that he had received from God (Hebrews 11:17–19; James 2:20–24). Abraham demonstrates that faith requires *humility*—we are at the mercy of God to speak to us; *passion*—we must commit our most cherished possessions to God; and *knowledge*—because we cannot trust and obey what we do not know.

Chapter 6

GOD

*You exist so truly, Lord my God, that You
cannot even be thought not to exist.*
ANSELM

Renowned atheist Christopher Hitchens debated theologian Doug Wilson in a written, six-part series entitled, "Is Christianity Good for the World?" Hitchens powerfully argued that Christianity has inflicted much evil upon the world, for it inspired Christians to support the Crusades, slavery, and anti-Semitism. After Hitchens's opening remarks, many readers may have felt sorry for Wilson. How could he deny that numerous atrocities had been committed in the name of Christ?

He didn't. Wilson agreed that Christians had done many bad things, but he wondered how an atheist such as Hitchens could claim they were bad. If there is no God, then who can say what is right or wrong? I may not want you to kill me, but I can't say you are wrong for doing so. I may appeal to my community, saying that society prefers you not kill me, but this still stops short of a moral law. Entire nations can behave badly, as every holocaust proves.

Only the existence of a personal absolute—a Grand Sez Who— is able to ground morality. An act is not evil merely because it offends me or my community, but because it angers a personal God who transcends us all. If God does not exist, then everything is permitted. You may not like an act, and that's your preference, but that's all it is. Without God, you cannot explain why anything is ultimately good or evil.

Wilson probed this moral problem by asking Hitchens, "When another atheist makes different ethical choices than you (as Stalin and Mao certainly did), is there an overarching common standard for all atheists that you are obeying and which they are not obeying? If so, what is the standard and what book did it come from? Why is it binding on them if they differ with you?"

Hitchens dodged this question in his subsequent responses. He repeated his charge that Christians had done bad things, but he could not say what standard they had violated. He finally concluded that "Our morality evolved. Just as we have. Natural selection and trial-and-error have given us the vague yet grand conception of human rights." Wilson replied that evolution is not a standard, for it teaches that reality is ever changing. He wrote, "If evolution isn't done yet (and why should it be?), then that means our morality is involved in this on-going flux as well. And that means that everything we consider to be 'moral' is really up for grabs. Our 'vague yet grand conception of human rights' might flat disappear just like our gills did."

Wilson also noted that when Hitchens declares that someone has acted immorally, he means to say more than that they are simply "less evolved." Hitchens isn't bothered by koala bears whose ears haven't evolved enough to stick close to their heads, but he is outraged by the evil he sees in the world. Evolutionary errors are often cute; moral errors are deeply offensive. We don't blame anyone for being less evolved, but we will lock them away for being less than moral. Doesn't this indicate that evolution and morality are not the same thing?

Wilson observed that few people display as much righteous indignation as Hitchens. He has preached vociferously against the evils of totalitarian regimes, but what gives him this right? Because

Hitchens rejects God, he has "great sermons but no way of ever coming up with a text." Wilson concludes that atheism not only gives the wrong answer to the question, Is Christianity good for the world?, but even worse, it fails to make sense of the question. He explains: "If Christianity is bad for the world, atheists can't consistently point this out, having no fixed way of defining 'bad.' If Christianity is good for the world, atheists should not be asked about it either because they have no way of defining 'good.'"

Your Stubborn Belief in God

The Wilson-Hitchens debate demonstrates a surprising fact about belief in God. Modern people often feel silly for saying they believe in God. What evidence do we have? Hasn't science shown that everything—including our idea of God—springs from entirely natural causes? But just when we think we may have to give up belief in God, we realize that it is impossible for anyone, even hard-core atheists such as Hitchens, to live as if God does not exist.

Besides the argument from morality, there is also an impressive case to be made from rationality. Everyone who claims to know something assumes at least two things: (1) their mind and senses are functioning properly and (2) their mind and senses are matched to this earthly environment. A person would doubt whatever he knows if he thought his mind was messed up or that his ears or eyes were not suited to reliably detect what happens in the world.

But what gives us confidence to believe that both (1) and (2) are true? Only God, and nothing else. Atheists rightly believe their minds are functioning properly, but they should probe deeper and ask why this is so. The only ground to believe that our minds are functioning properly and are suited for this environment is an intelligent Being who made both our minds and this world and then put them together. As C. S. Lewis explained, if God does not exist, then the entire world, including our minds, is the product of chance. But chance is irrational because it is random. This would mean that our rationality rests upon irrationality. But if our minds are the product of irrationality, why would we trust them?*

Here's the point: we assume God's existence every time we think, utter an intelligible sentence, or declare that some act is right or wrong. Everyone who relies on their minds and morality in this way assumes the existence of God. As even the skeptical Voltaire admitted, "If God did not exist, it would be necessary to invent Him."

Even the denial of God assumes His existence. Consider the sentence, "God does not exist." This is a logically coherent sentence, but what does that assume? The fact that it is logical points to the existence of logical laws. As with morality, these laws must be larger than any individual or group, for no one believes that individuals or groups have the right to create their own laws of logic. If a thief declares that he did and did not steal my wallet, I won't admire his creative use of the law of noncontradiction. I will tell the police to get my wallet back.

What transcends both me and the thief and grounds the laws of logic? What guarantees that logic is a law that both the thief and I must oblige? Only God, and nothing else. Thus, even a sentence that denies God's existence, insofar as it makes logical sense, is itself a conclusive argument for God's existence. We can't logically deny God's existence without also proving Him, and with the same argument. Saint Anselm said this is why Psalm 14:1 declares, "The fool says in his heart, 'There is no God.'" Only a fool would deny the existence of God with a sentence that assumes that very existence.

What You Can't Not Know

Perhaps these arguments still leave you with doubts. They may have convinced you that belief in God is rational but not that God

---

* Alvin Plantinga has extended this argument from rationality, arguing that materialistic naturalism (the dominant form of atheism) cannot possibly explain how our cognitive faculties are aimed at truth (rather than mere survival advantage) or even how the neural firings in our brains form beliefs that have cognitive content. If naturalism was true, we wouldn't be able to believe anything, including the belief that "naturalism is true." In this way naturalism is self-defeating.

is real. We may inevitably live as if God exists, but how do we know for sure that He does? This is a perceptive question, and it deserves an equally persuasive answer.

I could point to evidence from nature. Why is there something rather than nothing? And why is this something beautifully arranged, as if it was designed? We live on the razor's edge in a universe that is finely tuned for life. If the Earth orbited any closer to the sun we would burn up; if it inched farther away we would freeze. If gravity had been stronger or weaker than one part in 10^{40} (that is a ten with forty zeroes behind it), then life-sustaining stars such as our sun would not exist.

Or think small. Every time you scratch your skin, about ten skin cells flake off and become stuck beneath your fingernail. Each of these cells contains your entire genetic code, which if stretched out would fill three hundred Encyclopedia Britannicas (remember them?). Somehow each cell knows to read only the part of the code that pertains to its place in the body, and somehow for most of us this voluminous code is mostly spelled correctly. Just one typo in this three hundred book set—one wrong letter in the wrong place—may cause a debilitating disease or deformity.

But though "the heavens declare the glory of God" (Psalm 19:1), the evidence from nature is not the main reason why you believe in God. Here is how you can know for certain that God exists: *You just do.*

How is that persuasive?

Because you *know* that you do.

The apostle Paul declares that you, along with everyone else, know that God exists. He writes, "For since the creation of the world God's invisible qualities—his eternal power and divine nature—have been clearly seen, being understood from what has been made, so that men are without excuse." Paul says that God has made His existence "plain" to everyone, so no one can stand before God and say they honestly didn't know about Him (Romans 1:19–20). Many may plead ignorance, but they don't have an excuse that God will accept. He knows they know better.

God knows you know Him because He created you in His image. Every time you look in a mirror you see a reflection of God. Every time you think logically or act morally you brush against the character of God, who is the source of logic and morality. You cannot lose this knowledge of God because you never learned it. It is innate, lying so deep within your heart that no doubt or distress can ever dig it out. From birth, as your mind developed and became self-aware, you recognized you were already aware of another Self.* As John Calvin observed,

> There is within the human mind, and indeed by natural instinct, an awareness of divinity. This we take to be beyond controversy. To prevent anyone from taking refuge in the pretense of ignorance, God himself has implanted in all men a certain understanding of his divine majesty. Ever renewing its memory, he repeatedly sheds fresh drops.

Still, you may remain troubled. This discussion may seem too abstract and academic. It has convinced you that you should believe in God, and maybe that deep down you already do, but you just don't feel it. How can you *know* that you know God exists?

Maybe it will help to work the problem from the other direction. I dare you to persuade yourself that God does not exist. Try to make yourself not believe in God, if only for a moment. Tell yourself there is no God, no one who created and redeemed you, no one to raise you from the dead. You live, you die, and then you disappear, never to be seen or heard from again. Try to make yourself accept as fact that God does not exist. I bet you can't do it.

---

* Because Romans 1:18 says that sinners "suppress the truth" of God, one philosopher suggests that Paul is claiming that "sin has left people without a belief in God." Their sin prevents some people from honestly knowing that He exists. I disagree. Suppression requires a minimal level of knowledge, for we can't suppress something that isn't there. Our suppression certainly hinders us from learning more about God, but its existence assumes that we know enough to suppress. We may be quite ignorant of God, but it's our fault. Chapter 11 will address this problem of unbelief. Here I examine the foundational knowledge that sin can never entirely uproot.

Did a wave of nausea just wash over you? Did you break into a cold sweat and find that you had to sit down? Did you protest, "No! I do believe in God! I must believe in God!"

If you didn't respond like this, try the experiment again. Say "There is no God" out loud, so you can feel the full brunt of this belief. Or take the experiment one step further, and try to *live* as if God does not exist. This is even more difficult, for every meaningful word and deed implies Him. You can say, "Life has no meaning," but if you mean something by that already you are assuming that God exists.

For the rest, your cry of despair indicates that belief in God is not within your control. You may have doubts about God's existence, but you are powerless to stop believing in Him. You may live in a secular age, surrounded by people who insist that the evidence for God is inconclusive. You may often feel overwhelmed by their arguments and completely clueless about how to respond. But even now, in this toxic environment for faith, when you stop to think about it, you realize rather quickly that you still believe in God. It's impossible not to.

Deep down everyone believes in God, even outspoken atheists like Christopher Hitchens. When Hitchens died of esophageal cancer, his debate opponent and now friend Douglas Wilson wrote a eulogy. He noted that Hitchens tried to preempt a potential deathbed conversion by saying that if he should become a believer in his last days, that would only prove he was no longer in his right mind. Wilson said it was interesting that Hitchens did not merely warn that a Christian nurse might spread lies about his last-ditch conversion. He warned that he might actually do it. Hitchens was alerting his atheist friends that after a lifetime of passionate unbelief, his faith in the absence of God might fail in the end. He realized that belief in God would always be a live option, even more as he approached death.

Perhaps you are persuaded that you do believe in God. But with all the candidates claiming to be God, how do you know you have the right One? We examine this question next.

Chapter 7

JESUS

I know whom I have believed, and am
convinced that he is able to guard what
I have entrusted to him for that day.
PAUL THE APOSTLE

Chuck Colson pulled his car to the side of the road, buried his face in his hands, and sobbed. As special counsel to the president, Colson was proudly known as "Nixon's hatchet man," a loyal soldier who would "walk over his own grandmother if he had to." President Nixon admired his high skills and low scruples, and he learned to trust Colson with dirty jobs, such as smearing the reputation of a political opponent or war protestor. Colson didn't think twice about the morality of such tactics. He was intoxicated by his access to the Oval Office, weekends at Camp David, and grudging respect of his enemies.

But his world was beginning to unravel. The previous year burglars had broken into the offices of the Democratic National Committee in the Watergate building. The criminals were linked to Howard Hunt, who had worked with Colson in the Nixon White House. Colson knew nothing of the burglary and thought it was silly when he first heard of it, but many in Washington assumed it was his idea. The break-in did sound like something he might do, and soon enough he was indicted. Not long after that he would cop a plea and go to prison.

Now, as the net was closing in, Colson drove home from a visit with Tom Phillips, the president of Raytheon. Phillips had recently been saved at a Billy Graham Crusade, and he told Colson how Jesus had filled the emptiness of his ostensibly successful life. He said he knew that Colson had the same need, for he wouldn't resort to dirty tricks if he knew his cause was just. Phillips said, "Chuck, I don't think you will understand what I'm saying about God until you are willing to face yourself honestly and squarely. This is the first step." Then he read a chapter on pride from C. S. Lewis's *Mere Christianity*, said a prayer, and sent Colson on his way with a copy of the book.

Colson had barely left the driveway when a torrent of tears forced him to pull off. He knew that Phillips had hit the target. His pride had led him into this trap, and only Jesus could pull him out. He prayed, "God, I don't know how to find you, but I'm going to try! I'm not much the way I am now, but somehow I want to give myself to you." He didn't know what else to say, so he simply repeated the words, "Take me."

The next morning Colson and his wife left for vacation in Maine. He took along *Mere Christianity*, and for the better part of a week he wrestled with the claims of Jesus. Would he submit to Jesus as Lord of his life? He knew that to say "Not now" was really to say "No," and so on Friday morning he stared at the sea and prayed, "Lord Jesus, I believe you. I accept you. Please come into my life. I commit it to you."

And he did. Colson's conversion created a media firestorm, and many scoffed at its convenient timing. No one is laughing now. After his release from prison, Colson established the ministry Prison Fellowship, wrote numerous books, and even returned to the White House. As a confidant of George W. Bush, Colson encouraged political initiatives to end the war in Sudan, halt sex trafficking, and prevent the spread of HIV/AIDS. By the time of his death, Colson was esteemed as an evangelical elder statesman.

Colson's story is an enduring testimony to the matchless power of the grace of Christ. Other religions may have conversion stories, but none could solve Colson's problem of sin. Consider if Tom Phillips had been Buddhist. He would have told Colson that pride and the pain it caused are merely an illusion, a reminder that all of life is suffering and nothing here is real. He must strive to let go of all desire so that one day he might disappear into the void of nirvana. If Phillips had been Hindu, he might have said something similar, with an emphasis on finding God within.

If Phillips had belonged to the New Age, he would have reminded Colson that he is God and must reassert his divine powers over the world. He is master of his own fate; no one can take him down unless he lets them. If Phillips had been Muslim, he would have urged Colson to commit himself to the five pillars of Islam and pray that is enough to satisfy the holy standards of Allah. Because Allah is merciful, he may put his thumb on the scale so that Colson's good works outweigh his bad. So Colson must halfway humble himself, enough to admit he needs some help but not so far that he cannot contribute to his salvation.

Some of these solutions are better than others, but none could transform Colson like the love of Christ. Only Jesus offers precisely what Colson knew he needed. Here's why.

What Every Person Knows They Need

In the opening chapter of his letter to the Romans, Paul declares that every person knows two facts about God. First, everyone knows that God is *almighty*, "for since the creation of the world God's invisible qualities—his eternal power and divine nature—have been clearly seen" (1:20). Second, everyone knows that God is *all righteous*, for "although they know God's righteous decree that those who do such things deserve death, they not only continue to do these very things but also approve of those who practice them" (1:32).

If everyone without exception knows that God is almighty and "alrighty," what should we logically conclude about ourselves? *We are not.* If we thought about it for a moment, we would realize we are in big trouble with this holy and omnipotent God, for we can never do enough to make up for our rebellion and satisfy His infinitely high demands. Any good deeds that we might do are deeds we already owe Him, so it's impossible to earn extra credit and atone for our sin. We are sunk.

What should we logically conclude we need? *Grace.* Not just a little bit, not just a boost, but the whole shebang. We need more than a hand up, we need a handout. Paul says we are "dead in [our] transgressions and sins" (Ephesians 2:1), so we can't begin to make the first move toward God or contribute the smallest bit to our salvation. It will take a work of God, from start to finish, if we are going to avoid hell and live forever.

How many candidates are there for this job? *Only one.* Every religion except Christianity encourages us to earn our own way, either by doing enough good works to satisfy a deity, meditating our way to enlightenment, or recognizing the well-hidden truth that we are God. Every other religion claims that we can partly save ourselves. Only Christianity teaches that just as it is cruel to cheer a corpse into action ("Get up! I believe in you!"), so it is mean to expect us to lift a finger to help ourselves. Only God can save us now.

And Christians believe that He did. This is a sublime mystery of the gospel: the story of what God did to save us is nothing we could have figured out beforehand. Who could have guessed that God would send His own Son to die for our sin so that we might live with Him? This surprising story turns on absurdities: God became a creature? God died? The Father abandoned His only Son? Even the most imaginative science fiction writer would be too embarrassed to float this plot. And yet the story resonates with what we desperately know we need, so that when we hear it we say, "Of course. If God was going to save us, this is precisely how He would have to do it." And if God is almighty and all righteous, He just might try.

The story of Jesus both shocks and satisfies: He is too unbelievable to be a human invention and yet He quenches the desperate yearnings of our souls. We could never dream Him up, yet we can't imagine living without Him. Jesus is so subversive He makes a virtue out of what many consider God's only vice: the problem of evil.

The Powerful Suffering of God

The problem of evil asks why an all-good and all-powerful God would allow evil to exist. If God is all good, He would not want evil, and if He is all powerful, He would be able to stop it. So why is there evil? This conundrum is the number-one reason people give for not believing in God, but actually it is the best reason to put our faith in Jesus. Christians cannot solve the problem of evil. No one can. But we can say more about it than anyone else.

Theism trumps atheism. It is logically impossible and psychologically devastating to believe in evil and not believe in God. It is logically impossible because the concept of evil is meaningless if God does not exist. If there is no God, the best I can say is that I dislike being robbed or getting cancer. I cannot say these events are evil, for what is bad for me might be good for someone else (whoever has my money or my job after I die). It is a bold move to declare "this is good" or "that is evil." Anyone who makes such judgments is assuming they know what is best for the entire world. But such knowledge lies only with God, so only He can tell us what is good and what is evil.

It is psychologically devastating because of the horror of believing that evil exists but not God. Consider the terror of believing in evil but not a God who can protect you from it. You believe that evil is randomly pinging around our world? What prevents you from becoming one of its victims? If you truly believe that evil exists, then you also need the security that only God can provide. You need the comfort of knowing He is not surprised by your mugging (moral evil) or medical diagnosis (natural evil) and He remains powerful enough to help you.

You may have significant doubts about God. But if you left your house today, if you passed an oncoming car without flinching, take these as signs that deep down you do believe there is a God who watches out for you. You don't ultimately believe you're subject to the whims of an irrational universe, but you live as if your life is kept in the hands of God. This is why, should tragedy strike, the first thing you'll do is pray.

Christianity trumps other theisms. Only a God can grant us *security* in the face of evil, and only the Christian God goes further and also *suffers* with us. The problem of evil is not an abstract problem for the Christian God. Our God doesn't ride above the fray, untouched by our fears and tears. He enters our world and joins our suffering to do something about it. We don't know why God has allowed evil to enter our world, but we do know He has allowed evil to get to Him.

No one has suffered more from evil than God. The worst evil that has ever occurred happened on the cross, when the innocent Son bore the guilt of the world and cried out in despair, "My God, my God, why have you forsaken me?" (Matthew 27:46). This moment was saturated with such unspeakable horror that even though Jesus knew it was coming and sweat blood as He braced himself for it, when the abandonment came it still crushed Him to hell. Few theologians have attempted to explain that awful moment, or even how it was possible. If the Father is in the Son and the Son is in the Father (John 17:21), then it is unthinkable that anything could come between them. The best explanation I've heard comes from Graham Cole, who said that the Holy Spirit, who is the bond of love that unites the Father and Son, grabbed both and with arms fully extended strained with all His might to keep the Godhead from splitting up. For one terrible and eternal moment it looked as if this could go either way. And all because of our sin.

The cross absorbed and exhausted the powers of evil. Satan threw everything he had at Jesus, who allowed the devil to take Him down so He could take him out. Jesus dragged sin, death, and Satan down with Him into the grave, and when He arose He left them in the dust.

The cross doesn't tell us why God allows all sorts of evil to enter His world, but it does assure us that we can trust Him with it. You and I know why Jesus died, which means we know the reason for the worst evil that has ever occurred. If we know *the reason* for the greatest evil, then surely we can trust God with the lesser, though significant, evils that happen to us. We don't have to know why this or that event happened. We know that God was still God at the cross, and so we can believe that He remains God in whatever evil we face.

And what kind of God is He? He is high above us, and so He grants us security. He has defeated the forces of darkness, which guarantees that we will ultimately triumph over evil. He is also here with us, close enough to weep and suffer with our pain. Jesus can "sympathize with our weaknesses," for He has endured whatever evil we will ever experience (Hebrews 4:15). When we cry out in agony to God, we cry out to a God who gets it. There is no pain you can suffer that He hasn't already felt, and more deeply. So "Cast all your anxiety on him because he cares for you" (1 Peter 5:7).

Do you believe in evil? That's the best reason I know to believe in Jesus. Only Jesus can supply the security, success, and sympathy that you know you need. No other religion even makes an offer. But how do you know Jesus is real? We examine that question next.

Chapter 8

BIBLE

My sheep listen to my voice;
I know them, and they follow me.
JESUS

Carl Sagan's novel *Contact*, made into a movie starring Jodie Foster, tells the story of Ellie Arroway's search for extraterrestrial intelligence (ETI). Ellie wrestled with the usual questions you'd expect: Do aliens exist? Would they be able and willing to speak to us? How would they communicate and what would they say? Ellie considered other factors. Perhaps they are not advanced enough to reach us, or they are so advanced they'd rather ignore us. Perhaps we are listening on the wrong frequency, at the wrong time, for the wrong thing.

One-by-one Ellie turned her antenna to forty-some stars, and then told her mentor she was ready to quit. "There's not a hint of a signal. Maybe there's no one out there. Maybe the whole business is a waste of time."

He replied, "But there's hundreds of billions of stars in the Galaxy. You've looked at only a handful. Wouldn't you say it's a little premature to give up?" He pressed, "This is the time to be optimistic. . . . Imagine them out there sending us signals, and nobody on Earth is listening. That would be a joke, a travesty. Wouldn't you be ashamed of your civilization if we were able to listen and didn't have the gumption to do it?"

Ellie plowed ahead, and several years later she detected a series of prime numbers that seemed to be coming from the star Vega. The signal contained layers of messages, one of which was construction instructions for a complex machine. The nations of the world united to build the machine and chose Ellie to try it out. The machine worked and transported Ellie through a series of wormholes to Vega, where she spoke to an alien who assumed the image of her deceased father.

When Ellie returned home, she learned that those running the experiment thought it had failed, for they saw the machine drop through its spinning rings into its safety net. Ellie had not even left the launch pad. When Ellie insisted she had spent the last eighteen hours on Vega, they replied that her fall had knocked her unconscious, and she had only been out for twenty minutes. Ellie had recorded her visit, but when she played the tapes she found they were nothing but static—though eighteen hours of it. And so Ellie had a new problem she hadn't considered when she began her search for ETI: If aliens do communicate with you, how can you go public and convince others of that fact?

Sagan's story is intriguing because he draws parallels between Ellie's claim that she found ETI and Christians' claim that we have received a revelation from God. Both God and extraterrestrials lie beyond our reach. If we are going to make contact, they must take the initiative and connect with us. And when they do, the person who receives the revelation may look ridiculous trying to convince those who don't have ears to hear. Ellie didn't believe her Christian friends who said they had a word from God, just as her science colleagues didn't believe she had actually gone to Vega. But she had, and they did.

The questions Ellie asked about ETI will helpfully frame our reflection on revelation. Can we expect God to communicate with us? What would His message be? And if God does speak to us, how would we know?

Would God Speak to Us?

Would God speak to us? In some ways this is a moot question because deep down everyone knows that He already has. As we learned in chapter 6, God has revealed to everyone that He is almighty and all righteous. But can we expect God to go beyond this general revelation and speak to us in special ways, such as through Jesus or the Bible? Of course. God does not need to speak to us to fill some void in His life. He was perfectly pleased before He made us, and He would remain contented had He chosen to ignore us. But since God is almighty, we know that He is able to speak to us. And since He is all righteous, we know that He probably would.

Let me explain. Righteousness isn't about rule keeping. It's about love, for the right thing to do is the loving thing. Jesus readily broke the rules—healing on the Sabbath, touching unclean lepers—when love required it. This is not a surprise. Jesus is a member of our triune God, who is a community of self-giving lovers. God is a Father, Son, and Holy Spirit, three persons who continually set aside what might be in their own interest to serve the others. This is why Jesus prayed, "Not my will, but yours be done" (Luke 22:42), and the Spirit obeys both the Father and the Son (John 15:26). Because they lovingly serve each other, these divine persons thrive in their triune life. They embody the truth that "whoever loses his life for me will find it" (Matthew 16:25), for nothing is more alive than our self-giving God of love.

If our triune God is perfectly satisfied within himself, why did He bother to create our world? He wasn't lonely or looking for someone to talk with; He has all the fellowship He needs within His divine community. So creation isn't necessary. But neither is it a surprise. Given who God is—a community of persons who sacrificially love the others—it is fitting that God would allow His love to overflow His borders and create new others to love. Creation is an entirely appropriate act for a triune God. It's precisely what we might expect a loving God would do.

What about redemption? God didn't need to save us. Nothing in His nature required Him to rescue us from our sinful rebellion. But neither is our salvation a surprise. Given who God is—a community of persons who sacrificially love the others—it is fitting that God would willingly do whatever it takes to win us back. Redemption is an entirely appropriate act for a triune God. It's precisely what we might expect a loving God would do.

And what does redemption require? *Revelation*. It's impossible to save someone without communicating with them, especially if the rescue requires the savior to show up in person. This is precisely what the Bible says God did.

What Would God Say?

A loving God who decides to save us would do and say whatever it takes. He would send Jesus, "the Word" who "became flesh and made his dwelling among us" (John 1:14). The Word became flesh because our sin had dug a hole of debt we could not pay. Any good deed that we might offer is something God already deserved, so we could not earn extra credit to make up what we owed. Only the innocent Son of God, whose infinitely valuable life is sufficient to cover the sins of the whole world, could satisfy the demands of our holy God.

The Son entered our world to save us and show us what God is like. Jesus fully reveals God, for He "is the radiance of God's glory and the exact representation of his being" (Hebrews 1:3). Jesus both confirms and exceeds what everyone knows about God from nature. The life and death of Jesus assures us that God is love—just what nature taught us to expect from an all-righteous being—but it also promises that God is more loving than we ever dared to dream.

God would have loved if He had merely created us. He still would have loved if He had merely entered our world. But to endure ridicule, rejection, and the humiliating and excruciating death at the very hands of the people He came to save? And worse, to have His Father take their side and abandon Him? Who can begin to "grasp how wide and long and high and deep is the love of Christ," a "love that surpasses knowledge"? (Ephesians 3:18–19). This love compels typically cautious scholars to reach for superlatives. Alvin Plantinga is the most acclaimed philosopher of our generation, and he exclaims, "This overwhelming display of love and mercy is not merely the greatest story ever told; it is the greatest story that *could* be told" (emphasis his).

Which is just what we might have expected. God didn't make the effort to enter our world merely to repeat the stories we already have. He didn't come all this way to look around and say, "Carry on. You have everything under control. Keep up the good work." He came because He saw our hopeless despair, and He knew we needed something spectacular. His definitive Word—the only Word that saves you and then keeps on going—is Jesus.

How Can We Know That God Has Spoken?

We learn about Jesus from Scripture, which Jesus commissioned His apostles to write, under the direction of the Holy Spirit (John 16:12–15). So the most important question—the foundation that lies beneath "Would God speak to us?" and "What would He say?"—is how we know the Bible is God's Word. This is everything, because if the Bible is not a revelation from God, if it can't be trusted to tell us who God is and what He has done, then we have no hope to be saved.

Our belief in the Bible requires both humility and confidence. We must humbly admit that we cannot prove the Bible is the Word of God. We have lots of evidence that the Bible is a special book. It is full of wisdom, fulfilled prophecies, and historical facts that check out. It rings true with everything we know from science, literature, and psychology.* This evidence is important, because it would be difficult

---

* Science is a controversial area so let me explain further. God reveals himself through His Word and through His world. The content of these "two books" does not contradict, though our interpretation of each book may contain errors. When properly understood, what we learn from Scripture and what we learn from nature will agree. For example, natural science does not disprove the biblical account of miracles, for science merely describes the normal operation of nature. It cannot tell us what happens when a supernatural force directly intervenes in our world.

to believe the Bible is God's Word if it said things we knew were wrong. But no amount of evidence can prove the Bible is the Word of God. Many books are true, honest, and wise—I've written two of them (out of five!)—yet they don't rise to the level of God's speech.

It is impossible to prove God from below, so no evidence or argument can make someone cry uncle and concede that God wrote the Bible. This is a good thing, because if we could prove the Bible by appealing to a higher authority, then the Bible would no longer be our highest authority. What if God's Word is like God's existence, something we cannot prove but also do not have to, because it should be evident to all? John Calvin says that Scripture is self-authenticating, or obviously the Word of God to anyone who reads it. He writes, "Scripture exhibits fully as clear evidence of its own truth as white and black things do of their color, or sweet and bitter things do of their taste." Just as swans are indisputably white and sugar is undeniably sweet, so those who read Scripture should recognize that it is the voice of God.

But we don't. Just as we sinfully suppress our natural knowledge of God (Romans 1:18), so our sinful condition blinds us from seeing the Bible is God's Word. What we need, says Calvin, is the Holy Spirit to open our eyes to what we should have known all along. He explains, "For as God alone is a fit witness of himself in his Word, so also the Word will not find acceptance in men's hearts before it is sealed by the inward testimony of the Spirit. The same Spirit, therefore, who has spoken through the mouths of the prophets must penetrate into our hearts to persuade us that they faithfully proclaimed what had been divinely commanded."

Do you have doubts that the Bible is God's Word? Investigate the evidence for the Bible, such as its reliable manuscript tradition, the early and widespread support of the church, and the many martyrs who gave their lives to defend it. But realize from the outset that these facts will never be more than corroborating evidence. If my wife calls and tells me our house has burned down, the urgency in her voice is self-authenticating. At that moment I believe my house is gone. Because my wife is honest, I expect to find lots of evidence to support her report, such as a smoldering hole in the ground, when I get home. If I find the house standing in good condition, no worse for wear, I won't hug her and say, "You got me! What an invigorating sense of humor!" And I certainly won't believe the next time she cries wolf.

Thank God for the loads of evidence we have for the Bible, for it's just what we'd expect if the Bible is what it claims to be. But know that the only way you will know for sure the Bible is God's Word is to ask the Holy Spirit to speak to your heart while you read it. Put yourself in God's hands and see if He doesn't open your ears to hear His voice. I'm not saying the Spirit will tell you what the Bible means. That requires (and deserves!) careful attention and study. But I do expect Him to make it obvious that you are reading His Word. You may endure periods of silence, when the heavens seem to be impenetrable brass. But the God who sacrificed His only Son didn't go to all that trouble to blow you off now. So read the Bible in hope, believing His promise to reward "those who earnestly seek him" (Hebrews 11:6).

Here's a tip: the Spirit of Jesus is present whenever the church assembles for worship (Matthew 18:20; 1 Corinthians 5:4), so go to church. Listen to the Word proclaimed by a Spirit-anointed minister, and see if it doesn't become easier to believe the Bible is what it claims to be: the Word of God addressed directly to you (Matthew 22:31; 1 Corinthians 10:11; Hebrews 3:7–4:13). There is no need to flounder on your own. Get yourself to where God has promised to be.

As with Ellie and her discovery of ETI, you won't be able to prove to others that you have a revelation from God. But so what? Invite them to church, where you know the Spirit is present, or ask them to read the Bible for themselves. Start them out in the gospel of John, and pray that the same Spirit who opened your eyes will do the same for them. If He doesn't, there is not much you can do for them. You have done your job, for you have brought them to God. They are in His hands now, and I can't think of a more promising place to be.

Chapter 9

BELIEF

For I do not seek to understand so that I may believe;
but I believe so that I may understand.
ANSELM

This has gone on long enough. I've talked a lot about belief, knowledge, and doubt, but I haven't yet said what these words mean. It's time to define terms, not so we can impress people at dinner parties (or at least not *only* that) but so we can pinpoint the problem of doubt and plan a strategy for dealing with it.

You've probably already noticed that the term "belief" is used in two related but different ways. Consider these two statements:

"I believe it is going to rain today."

"I believe in God, the Father almighty, creator of heaven and earth."

In the first sentence "I believe" means "I think so," which is purposely less than saying "I know so." If I'm not sure it will rain today, I won't say I *know* it, but I may humbly declare I think it might. My belief is headed toward knowledge, for if it does rain and if I had good reasons to expect it, I might later revise my claim and boast that I *knew* it.

Philosophers who study these things often define knowledge as a justified true belief. We may claim to know something if and only if:

1. We believe it.
2. What we believe turns out to be true.
3. We have good reasons for believing it.

We may believe things that happen to be true (#2), but we only *know* them if our reasons for believing them are more than a lucky guess (#3). If I say I know it will rain because my fortune cookie warned of gathering storms, then whether it rains or not, no one would say that I *knew* it.

Notice two things about the everyday use of "belief" (#1). First, it requires some level of commitment. I may be unsure whether it is going to rain, but if I say I believe it will, then I have inclined myself in that direction. I have put myself on record, and now I run the risk of being wrong. Second, the commitment it requires is slight, and this by design. We say "I believe" when we want to dial back our claims to knowledge. If we're not confident that something is true, we may lower the temperature by saying we merely believe, or think it is. Conversely, when we're sure about what we believe, we won't settle for the word "belief." If you want to annoy a scientist, ask if he *believes* in evolution or global warming. I heard an interviewer innocently ask a climatologist, "Do you believe in climate change?" The scientist replied, "I wouldn't use the term 'belief,' because it's not that weak. I follow the evidence, so I *know*." Well, okay then.

This weak sense of "belief" is not what the Apostles' Creed means when it declares "I believe in God, the Father almighty, creator of heaven and earth." Christians who recite the creed aren't humbly trying to stay on this side of knowledge but are resolutely declaring that they have committed themselves to the God they know. Unlike the weak use of belief that *leans toward* knowledge, this strong sense of belief lies on the other side of knowledge and *leans on* it. In both cases "belief" means to commit, but the weaker version is headed toward knowledge while the stronger one comes after.

This chapter will use the term "faith" to distinguish the strong use of belief from its weaker cousin. This is a somewhat arbitrary decision, as faith can stand in for both phases of belief, but it will keep our terms straight. You may believe in just about anything—

note the many sports fans of losing teams who valiantly hold up signs that say "We believe"—but you should only *believe,* or have faith, in those who have proven worthy of your trust.

Such faith always comes as our response to what we know. The apostle Paul declares, "I *know* whom I have *believed,* and am *convinced* that he is able to guard what I have *entrusted* to him for that day" (2 Timothy 1:12). Paul's faith follows knowledge, for he believes in whom he knows and trusts what he is convinced of. As we learned in chapter 5, the Reformers said the commitment of faith (*fiducia*) requires a base of knowledge (*notitia* and *assensus*). The more certain we are of what we know, the more likely we are to give ourselves to it, which is the point after all. And so Martin Luther defined faith as "a living, daring confidence in God's grace, so sure and certain that the believer would stake his life on it a thousand times."

The following diagram captures what I've been saying and adds more. Take a moment to review it and then meet me on the other side for some important observations.

The Path of Belief and Its Challenges

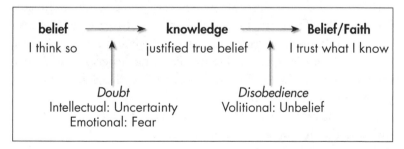

Beliefs about Belief

Faith Is Our Goal

No one is satisfied with the weak form of belief. The whole point of believing anything is to turn that belief into knowledge, which then can be trusted. This is especially true when it comes to God. James 2:19 declares, "You believe that there is one God. Good! Even the demons believe that—and shudder." Demons think that God exists, but they do not trust Him with their lives. We expect that from demons because well, they're demons, but God's people can do better. We must go all in, or what's believing for?

Faith Begins with Belief

We aren't satisfied with mere belief but we do value it. The weak sense of belief is not our goal, but our pursuit of faith cannot get started without it. It's impossible to fully give ourselves to someone or something we don't believe in. Hebrews 11:6 says, "Anyone who comes to [God] must believe that he exists and that he rewards those who earnestly seek him." We won't believe *on* God unless we first believe *in* Him, or think that He exists and hears our prayers.

A father once brought his demon-possessed son to be healed by Jesus. He had heard reports that Jesus could cast out demons, and he believed them enough to bring his child to Him. When he arrived he found that Jesus wasn't around, so he asked the disciples if they could help, and they tried and failed. Their failure shook his faith, and he began to wonder if he had gullibly swallowed the hype. By the time Jesus came down from the mountain, the father wasn't sure what to believe. He put his fears and frustration directly to Jesus: "But if you can do anything, take pity on us and help us."

Jesus caught the angst in the man's voice and replied, "*If you can*? . . . Everything is possible for him who believes." The father quickly corrected himself. "I do believe," he replied, "help me overcome my unbelief!" (Mark 9:22–24).

The father desperately wanted to believe that Jesus could help his son, but his experience with the disciples had raised some doubts. And now Jesus had flipped the script, telling the man that the only obstacle to his son's deliverance was the man's faith, not Jesus' power. So the father replied, by his words and actions, "I do believe. I am so confident in your ability that I brought my son here. But I've been disappointed, so help me overcome my unbelief! Please strengthen my confidence in you, enough that I will entrust my son to you, for you are my last hope. Help me to believe *in* You so I can believe *on* You."

Faith Influences Belief

The weak sense of belief is logically prior to faith. We trust only what we think is true. But our faith also impacts what we take as true, for what we look for often determines what we see. Jesus said, "If anyone chooses to do God's will, he will find out whether my teaching comes from God or whether I speak on my own" (John 7:17). If you aren't sure what to think about Jesus, study the Bible and other historical evidence that supports His claims. But above all try "the obedience that comes from faith" (Romans 1:5). Give yourself to Jesus, following His commands rather than your own desires, and you'll find it easier to believe that He is the Son of God. This in turn will make it easier to give yourself to Him, which in turn will make it easier to believe in Him, and so on.

Of course, the pivotal role of faith cuts both ways. Our faith influences what we believe, whether that is for the virtuous cycle of faith → belief → faith or for the vicious cycle of unbelief → doubt → unbelief. When Paul arrived in Rome he invited the Jewish leaders of the city to come hear about Jesus. At the end of the day "some were convinced by what he said, but others would not believe." Paul chalked up their doubts to their disobedience. He quoted the prophet Isaiah, who said that "this people's heart has become calloused; they hardly hear with their ears, and they have closed their eyes." Paul announced that God had put stony-hearted Israel on the shelf and would now send His gospel "to the Gentiles, and they will listen!" (Acts 28:23–28).

Sort of. In the Bible's very next chapter Paul accuses the Gentiles of suppressing what they know about God. He explains, "Although they knew God, they neither glorified him as God nor gave thanks to him, but their thinking became futile and their foolish hearts were darkened" (Romans 1:18–21). Elsewhere Paul observed that the Gentiles' hearts were as hard as the Israelites'. He warned the Ephesians to "no longer live as the Gentiles do, in the futility of their thinking. They are darkened in their understanding and separated from the life of God because of the ignorance that is in them due to the hardening of their hearts" (Ephesians 4:17–18). The Gentiles' "futile thinking" made it more difficult to believe in God, but this was their fault. Their ignorance was not innocent, for their doubts sprouted from the fertile soil of disobedience.

Unbelief Destroys Faith and Deserves Judgment

This brings us to a key distinction between doubt and willful unbelief. The latter is always sin, as bad as it gets, because it knowingly disobeys what is right. God does not hold us accountable for what we could not know, but He rightly expects us to obey what we do. James 4:17 explains, "Anyone, then, who knows the good he ought to do and doesn't do it, sins." Unbelief is the opposite of faith, for rather than entrust our lives to God, we knowingly reject His love and try to make our own way in the world.

Scripture often warns against the danger of unbelief. Hebrews 3:12 cautions: "See to it, brothers, that none of you has a sinful, unbelieving heart that turns away from the living God." We must not follow the example of Israel, which was "not able to enter" the Promised Land and now is entirely "broken off because of unbelief" (Hebrews 3:19; Romans 11:20). If they do not repent, they will be thrown with the other "unbelieving" into "the fiery lake of burning sulfur," where they will languish forever with "the vile, the murderers, the sexually immoral, those who practice magic arts, the idolaters and all liars" (Revelation 21:8). Unbelief keeps bad company and promises a worse destiny.

Doubt Hinders Belief and Deserves Sympathy

The situation is different with doubt. Some doubts arise from unbelief, but many are honest attempts to figure out what is right. Such doubt is not the willful rejection of what we know is true but the haunting hesitation about what we think is true. Several of the New Testament's terms for doubt mean to hesitate between two paths (*distazō*) or to be divided between two minds (*diakrinō* and *dipsukos*). This is an apt description, for every doubter knows the turmoil of being stuck between reasons for and against something. We literally can't make up our minds.

Living in two minds is a problem. James 1:6–8 states, "He who doubts is like a wave of the sea, blown and tossed by the wind. . . .

He is a double-minded man, unstable in all he does." But unlike unbelief, which earns God's judgment, doubt receives His sympathetic shoulder. Jude 22 commands us to "Be merciful to those who doubt." As Jesus graciously stooped to give Thomas the evidence he demanded, so doubters need our compassion rather than condemnation (John 20:24–29).

We are kind to doubters because we know the next time it could be us. No matter how charmed your life has been or how many miracles you have seen, your faith is never entirely safe from doubt. Even some of the disciples who saw the resurrected Christ weren't immediately convinced. Matthew 28:17 says, "When they saw him, they worshiped him; but some doubted."

Don't be surprised by doubt. Prepare for it. The next chapter will show you how.

Chapter 10

QUEST

*We cannot imagine any certainty that is
not tinged with doubt, or any assurance
that is not assailed by some anxiety.*
JOHN CALVIN

Let's review. So far I've explained why it often seems hard to believe
in God, how modern people make matters worse by separating
faith from knowledge, and how the way forward is to put our faith
in what we know. I then explored what we know about God, Jesus,
and Scripture. These chapters were not exhaustive—I don't pretend to have covered every question—but they aimed to encourage
you that you already know more than you might think. You can't
stop knowing there is a God, and you have thick, sturdy reasons to
believe that Jesus is His Son and the Bible is His Word.

This is good to know, but it won't necessarily remove all doubt.
You may watch a documentary about the Muslim pilgrimage to
Mecca and wonder whether other religions, each in its own way,
also lead to God. You may hear an archaeologist claim he's discovered an ossuary that once held the bones of Jesus, and begin to
ponder the implausibility of the resurrection. You may lose a child
to cancer or a freak accident and angrily question how a loving God
could allow it.

Such doubts are not the sinful flailing of unbelief but the very human failing of your quest for knowledge. You desperately want to believe in Jesus, you just aren't sure you can. You're stuck in the wilderness between the Egypt of unbelief and the Promised Land of faith, knowing too much to go back and doubting too much to go on. The desert of doubt is no place to live—it's a doorway rather than a destination—but its temporary trials can strengthen your faith. As with other struggles in life, the key to surviving your doubts is attitude. Chuck Swindoll wisely said that life is 10 percent what happens to you and 90 percent how you respond to it. Honest doubts will happen to you. This is how to respond.

Be Thankful

No one enjoys doubt, but there are at least three reasons why everyone should thank God for it. First, doubt proves *you're honest.* Doubts are accountants in the business of faith. Successful corporations need visionary leaders to dream up fresh products and programs. But they also need number crunchers to keep them honest by asking, "How will we pay for this?" Without the former, a business will stagnate; without the latter, it will go bankrupt.

Likewise, our business of faith requires bold vision to pursue the ultimate questions of origins, meaning, and destiny. Whether we believe that an eternal God created this world from scratch or that it evolved out of nowhere on its own steam, the question isn't whether we will believe a fantastic story but which fantastic story will we believe? We shouldn't be shocked to find ourselves believing something incredible, for we are straining to understand the universe, from beginning to end and everything in between. Doubts will arise if we are doing this right, because who dares to think they have unlocked all the secrets of the universe? If it's been a long time since you entertained a serious doubt, it may mean that you are happily secure in the strong hands of God, or it could mean that you have simply stopped thinking.

Be thankful for your doubts, for they prove you aren't gullibly swallowing the company line, whether from your church or your culture, but you are trying to be a responsible believer. And whatever you do come to believe, you will hold that belief with passion and confidence.

Second, doubt indicates *you're a believer.* Doubt can be debilitating, especially when it claws at our most cherished beliefs. Doubt leaves us afraid and ashamed: we're scared that we're losing our faith and embarrassed that others might find out. This is a good time to remember that doubt means to exist in two minds. Doubt is not the fixed stand of unbelief, but the stumbling pursuit of faith. We lurch between faith and unbelief, praying we'll land on faith but unable to make up our minds. We're undecided, which means that at some level we still believe.

And the fact that we're troubled means we still believe a lot. You may doubt many things, such as whether you ordered the best sandwich on the menu, are wearing sensible shoes, or will win the next game of checkers. These doubts are real but they don't bother you much. You could be wrong about them all and not lose any sleep. But the doubts that trouble you are the agonizing questions that attack what you care about most. That pit in your stomach is proof that the belief under assault matters to you, which is evidence that you remain committed to it. If you take doubt as evidence that you no longer believe, then you must also take the alarm that accompanies it as proof that you still do.

Third, doubt means *you're normal.* The large decisions of life always come with various levels of doubt. Who has ever married or purchased a house and not wondered, if just a little and for a moment, if they were doing the right thing? Anyone who doesn't have any doubts on their wedding or closing day simply isn't paying attention.

Doubt is inevitable on the big ticket items, even when you've done your homework. Diligent investigation may remove all intellectual doubt, but you still must face the trauma of emotional doubt. For instance, I have no intellectual qualms with bungee jumping, beyond the obvious, "Are you crazy?" I may watch previous jumpers and come to believe that this bungee rope is strong (and short) enough to keep me alive. But that doesn't mean I'm jumping. I will still be overwhelmed by what psychologists call "the aspirational and ontological variance of the existential," or what normal folks call "fear."

As I stand on the ledge I will be crippled with experiential doubt. Sure, the bungee held the last thousand times, but it still might snap on my turn. Why would I trust my life to something with such a silly name? Is there a more undignified way to die? Just try and say "Death by bungee" with a straight face. If you ever hear that I tied a rope around my waist and leapt off a bridge, you can be sure that I was pushed.

In the same way, I may have no intellectual problems with God, at least for the moment. I may be more certain of His existence than I am of my own. I may believe all the stories in the Bible. But I still must face my fears and trust Him with my life. He may have saved thousands of believers in the past, but what if He fails on my turn? Diligent study may remove most, if not all, of our intellectual doubts, but nothing can eliminate all of our fears. At some point we're going to have to jump, or ask for a push.

Doubt is a regular part of our experience. Because we are *finite*, we won't ever know everything about anything, and because we are *fallen*, we're liable to mess up even what we should know (I'll cover this in the next chapter). So don't be surprised to find yourself doubting. It may just mean you're honest, faithful, and normal.

Stay Hopeful

Of course this will be little consolation if we lose hope of ever resolving our doubts. Who cares about being honest if it turns out we're honestly wrong? It's not enough to congratulate ourselves for having the courage to doubt; we must also roll up our sleeves and attempt to answer it. But we'll only do that if we believe our hard work has a good chance to pay off.

You may be inspired to wade into your doubts when you remember that your journey will end in three possible outcomes: you discover you were wrong and change your belief; you discover you were right and confirm your belief; or you can't determine what is right and wrong and so remain ambivalent. I'll give examples of each and conclude with help on the last, because that one's a bummer.

The young Martin Luther struggled with doubts about his salvation. He believed that entering a monastery would earn God's approval, but once there he wondered how he could ever become pure enough to satisfy a holy God. He badgered his confessor with trivialities or nonexistent sins until he was told to come back when he had actually done something wrong. Luther explained that his tormented "conscience would never give me assurance, but I was always doubting and said, 'You did not perform that correctly. You were not contrite enough. You left that out of your confession.'"

When in Rome he learned that he could free his grandfather from purgatory if he climbed the Santa Scala, twenty-eight "Holy Stairs" where Jesus purportedly stood before Pilate. Luther climbed the stairs on his knees, saying a prayer on each step, but when he got to the top he asked, "Who knows if it is really true?" Years later he encountered Johannes Tetzel, a travelling indulgence seller who told peasants, "As soon as the coin in the coffer rings, the soul from purgatory springs." Luther doubted that salvation could be bought and that the pope knew such chicanery occurred in his name, so he wrote down Ninety-five Theses to open a dialogue.

Luther's doubts unleashed a firestorm of criticism. He soon was expelled from the church, disowned by his spiritual father, and banned by the emperor. He hid for his life and battled personal attacks from opponents and quite possibly the devil, but he fought through it and came out the other side with a fresh recovery of the gospel. If Luther had stifled his doubts, he would not have discovered the liberating truth that we are justified by grace alone through faith alone, and you and I might still be trying to buy our salvation.

Sometimes Luther's doubts led him to double down on what he already believed. When Luther appeared before the emperor, the examiner asked if he wished to recant anything in the books he had written. He was a single monk standing against more than a thousand years of church tradition. What made him think he was right? Luther asked for time to reflect on this doubt and was given one day. The next evening when asked if he had made up his mind,

Luther responded, "Unless I am convinced by the testimony of the Scriptures or by clear reason . . . I am bound by the Scriptures I have quoted and my conscience is captive to the Word of God. I cannot and I will not retract anything, since it is neither safe nor right to go against conscience. May God help me. Amen."

Luther's struggles with doubt ended well, but what to do when there is no end in sight? How should you respond when you see reasons for and reasons against, and neither side seems to be winning? As a professor, I see this struggle in some of my students in regard to Luther. They are troubled by scholars who say that Luther misunderstood what the apostle Paul wrote about salvation. Other theologians defend Luther's view, with equally powerful arguments. As a result some students feel disorienting vertigo. They aren't sure how to read Paul's epistles or what to believe about salvation, and they know they need to find out.

They can remain calm in their quest if they remember to drill down, pounding their pylon of faith as deep as is necessary until they hit the bedrock of assured belief. They may have doubts about how to read Paul's epistles, but they are sure his epistles are God's Word. If they have doubts about this, they may go down one more level to their certainty that God exists. If they doubt God's existence, they may dig deeper (or perhaps sideways) to the obvious truth that they exist. If they question their own existence, then I must ask them, "Who is it that I'm speaking to?" Just try to answer that question while denying your existence.

Once they find their one true thing, the students can make this belief their foundation and build from there. As I explained in chapters 6–8, our own existence requires the existence of God, and the character of God offers compelling reasons for taking the Bible as His Word. So we should be able to believe in Scripture, especially if we have received the witness of the Spirit, and once there we may put our minds at ease as we investigate what Paul means.

Most of my students have worked through their vertigo and concluded that Luther got Paul mostly right. They are committed to preaching the Reformation gospel of grace alone through faith alone, now even more firmly because of their ordeal. Any who are still searching must rest in what they know—that Scripture is God's Word—and trust that all will be made clear, if not now, then when Jesus returns and their faith is made sight.

No one enjoys the desert of doubt, but we may respond with hope and gratitude because we know that doubt is not necessarily the enemy of faith. Disobedience is, and we examine that next.

Chapter 11

UNBELIEF

I hope there is no God! I don't want there to be a God;
I don't want the universe to be like that.
THOMAS NAGEL

When faith is firing on all cylinders, we enthusiastically commit to what we know to be true. We are sure that God exists, the Bible is His Word and Jesus is His Son, and we cheerfully entrust our lives to them all. We skip beneath sunny skies, whistling "'Tis So Sweet to Trust in Jesus." Until tragedy strikes. Anyone who has suffered through divorce, disease, or the death of a beloved can tell you that they can't express the depth of their fear and anguish. They are ambushed by doubts that scramble lifelong beliefs about God, the world, and their place in it.

But many will also tell you that these doubts do not destroy their faith. They breathe in, breathe out, and continue to believe in their faithful Savior, Jesus Christ. They find solace in the gritty faith of Job, who declared from his despair, "Though he slay me, yet will I hope in him" (Job 13:15). They make up their minds that their faith might rattle but it will not be rolled. So they pledge with Job, "When he has tested me, I will come forth as gold" (Job 23:10).

Doubt may knock faith off balance, because it casts suspicion on the knowledge we need to believe. But doubt need not cause our faith to fall. Faith means to commit, and we are still able to do that when we don't know for sure. If that wasn't the case, no one would ever marry, fly an airplane, or buy season tickets for Cleveland sports teams.

Doubt may give a glancing blow to faith, but unbelief is a direct hit. Unbelief damages faith in two ways. It destroys faith directly because it is its exact opposite. We can't rely on our knowledge of God when we reject what we know about Him and His will for us. Unbelief also hinders faith indirectly, for it breeds doubts that diminish the knowledge that faith needs to believe. This indirect challenge of unbelief is more subtle than its direct, in-your-face assault, and for that reason it may be even more dangerous. Some doubts are honest attempts to follow the truth wherever it leads, but others are devious efforts to fend off the truth whenever it comes. Let's find out how to tell the difference.

The Conflict of Faith and Unbelief

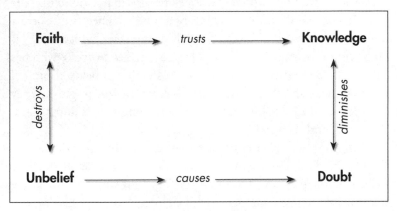

Doubts about Doubt

We must always be at least a little suspicious of doubt, for while not all doubt is sin, all doubt does come from sinners. Sinners have

an ax to grind. We are not morally neutral. We have a vested interest in disproving Jesus, for if He is Lord, then we can't be. Karl
Barth observed that we are tempted to raise a "technical difficulty"
to avoid the hard truth that Jesus has displaced us from the throne
of our lives. We realize "our hour has struck, our time has run its
course, and it is all up with us," so we pretend we're not convinced.
We ask how we can know for sure that Jesus is God, that He died
for our sins and rose from the dead. As long as there is room to
doubt, we suppose we're off the hook, excused to live as we please.

Some doubters do this openly and without apology. In *The Making of an Atheist: How Immorality Leads to Unbelief,* James Spiegel
documents how famous atheists, such as Percy Shelley, Bertrand
Russell, and Jean-Paul Sartre, raised doubts about God not because
that is where the evidence led but because it freed them to be sexually promiscuous. Aldous Huxley conceded that atheism robs the
world of meaning, but he argued that was a small price to pay for
the freedom to sleep with whomever you want. He wrote: "For
myself as, no doubt, for most of my contemporaries, the philosophy
of meaninglessness was essentially an instrument of liberation. The
liberation we desired was . . . liberation from a certain system of
morality. We objected to the morality because it interfered with our
sexual freedom."*

Likewise, philosopher Mortimer Adler acknowledged that
despite his intellectual arguments against belief in God, the real
reason he spent most of a lifetime refusing to believe was because
it "would require a radical change in my way of life, a basic altera-
tion in the direction of day-to-day choices as well as in the ultimate
objectives to be sought or hoped for. . . . The simple truth of the
matter is that I did not wish to live up to being a genuinely religious
person."

By their own admission unbelievers often know what they're
doing when they raise doubts about God. As Huxley explained,

---

* Notice how Huxley and his contemporaries illustrate the sinful slide described in Romans
  1:18–32. Paul explains that those who suppress their knowledge of God typically express
  their rebellion in sexual sin. Idolatry is the root sin and sexual immorality is the gateway
  sin that inexorably leads to a "depraved mind."

"We don't know because we don't want to know. It is our will that decides how and upon what subjects we shall use our intelligence. Those who detect no meaning in the world generally do so because, for one reason or another, it suits their books that the world should be meaningless."

Not all unbelievers are so self-aware. Some have so thoroughly suppressed their knowledge of God that they take their unbelief as a sign of virtue. In *Philosophers Without Gods*, Joseph Levine describes his journey to atheism and why he now thinks it's morally wrong to believe in God. Levine was raised in an orthodox Jewish home that studied Torah and strictly observed the Sabbath and kosher laws. But his home was located in Los Angeles in the 1960s, and before Levine left high school he had adopted the anti-authoritarian attitude of his hippie friends.

After graduation Levine tried to return to his Jewish roots, even studying the Torah in hopes of becoming a rabbi, but he couldn't get past the heavy-handed aspects of his religion. Levine wanted the freedom to question all authority, and he chafed beneath the stricture that "the Torah had to be right and you couldn't question God's Word." He believed in the equality of all people, and he was offended that God had raised the Jews above other nations. These moral problems with Judaism softened Levine to the philosophical arguments against God, and soon he realized that he could no longer believe in a "supernatural, omnipotent, omniscient, and omnibenevolent deity that created and watches over the world."

Unlike Huxley who brazenly used his doubts as an excuse to be immoral, Levine argues that his doubts are his moral duty. He writes that it's immoral to believe in God, for "belief in God expresses a rejection, or denial, or perhaps subjugation of one's humanity. It involves turning one's back on the human will to overcome challenges, to create, and instead makes servility to authority the ultimate aim of human life. . . . Why is it wrong? It's a sin against ourselves, that's why."

Notice that Levine keeps the religious concept of sin even as he discards the idea of God. But sin doesn't make sense in a world without God, so Levine steps in to take His place. Sin is no longer an offense against God but an offense against Me. And if I am the ultimate decider of right and wrong, then I am free to do whatever I want. And that's the point.

Levine ends up in the same place as Huxley but without Huxley's self-awareness, for what Huxley takes as license to sin Levine takes as his moral duty. He has reached the cockeyed cul-de-sac of unbelief, in which evil is mistaken for good and vice versa (Isaiah 5:20). Levine honestly thinks he is morally obligated to doubt God's existence, but he is not as honest as he thinks, for his doubts arise from the double move of self-deception.

Fool Me Twice

Self-deception is an impossibly difficult maneuver to pull off, yet every sinner quickly learns to master it. We tell ourselves that we stretched the truth not for our own benefit but to make the other person feel better, and we actually come to believe it. We say that our affair, addiction, or embezzlement is for the good of others, and we believe that too. We create our own versions of reality, pretend that we didn't, and then foolishly swallow both parts. We are our own dupes. To paraphrase Cornelius Plantinga Jr., self-deception requires us to make a move on ourselves and then cover up our tracks. We knowingly deceive ourselves, and then deceive ourselves into thinking we didn't.

This double move is precisely how doubt sprouts from unbelief. Unbelief is willful rebellion against God. Who would cop to that? If we plan to continue our rebellion, we'll need to conceal our sin beneath a thick smoke screen of intellectual problems. So we say that of course we'd obey God if we knew for sure who He was. It's not our fault that He hasn't made himself obvious or that the leading candidates for the one true religion often contradict each other and our sense of morality. All we can do is stay true to ourselves, following the dictates of our own hearts rather than the teachings of some domineering religion. And just like that, we trick ourselves into believing we don't know there is a God, and that we deserve a gold star for honesty.

Not all doubt comes from unbelief, but given our capacity for self-deception, how can we tell the difference? We may think our doubts are honest, but maybe we're just deceiving ourselves. Here's a tip: if unbelief is disobedience, then the doubts that are born from unbelief will be found in the home of disobedience, sharing a room with self-deception. As James urges, "Do not merely listen to the word, and so deceive yourselves. Do what it says" (James 1:22). If self-deception arises from disobedience, then you can tell you're on the trail of self-deception when you spy the tracks of disobedience.

Look for the obvious signs that enveloped Huxley: Is there something or someone that you would have to give up if you believed the Bible was true? Perhaps it's a person you know you shouldn't be dating, a practice you know you shouldn't be doing, or a possession you know God wouldn't want you to have, at least not now and in this way. If the price of obeying God is higher than you are willing to pay, that is a red flag that your doubts are not entirely honest. You may not be as open-minded as you think; you may just be cheap.

Also look for the more subtle signs that surrounded Levine. You may not be committing outright sin, but are you omitting good spiritual hygiene? Have you stopped going to church, praying, and reading Scripture? If you aren't paying attention to where God speaks, you shouldn't be surprised when you don't hear His voice. Like Levine with his hippie friends, we tend to adopt the values and attitudes of those who are closest to us. Our doubts are often social and emotional long before they become intellectual. If we hang with anti-authoritarian free spirits, we shouldn't be surprised when we feel suffocated by the limits laid out in God's Word. And when we disobey what we know is from God, it won't be long until we begin to doubt what we used to know. Either that, or we'll have to admit we are terrible people who hate God telling us what to do. Most people would rather doubt. It's easier and we look better doing it.

If unbelief is a leading cause of doubt, a leading remedy is a life of faith. Let's look at that next.

Chapter 12

DISCIPLINES

*Pray for the gift of faith, for the power to go on believing
not in the teeth of reason but in the teeth of lust and
terror and jealousy and boredom and indifference.*
C. S. LEWIS

I jogged four miles today, and I'll probably do it again tomorrow, because I just returned from visiting family in Ohio. My brother runs marathons, and every time I see him he's talking about his next race, rising before dawn to train for it, and inviting me to jog with him. I decline because he runs too far, too fast, and too early, but I return home inspired, determined to make room in my life for running, which I do for a while. My enthusiasm turns cold with the weather, and soon I'm swamped by a new semester of research, grading, and appointments, and I discover I'm too busy to exercise much. About that time I go to Ohio for the holidays, and I return with a new pair of running shoes.

Anything that requires effort requires a team. Even tasks that *can* be done in isolation often *won't* be done without a group. This is why aspiring authors join a writing club, learners go to school, and runners jog with friends. There is a name for marathoners who train alone: they're called spectators. Successful marathoners need the encouragement, accountability, and shared expertise that come from a team. I may not know how to stretch before and after a race, but if you do, you can help me. You may not know what to do when the bear climbs on your back at mile eighteen, but if I've been there, I can coach you through it. Neither of us wants to beat the sun out of bed, so we need each other for that too.

Left to myself in the dreary tundra of a Michigan winter, I lose sight of my goal and look for reasons not to run. The roads are icy and the health club is far away. Better stay home and write that chapter on spiritual discipline, the one that begins with the benefits of running. I probably should get out, but why make the effort? Throw on a loose sweater and no one will know the difference.

My running regimen suffers from sloth, which happens to be one of the seven deadly sins. Sloth means more than mere laziness. The church fathers described sloth with the Greek term *acedia*, which means apathy or indifference. Apathy is the evil root that produces laziness. We become lazy when we don't care, and we don't care when we lose hope. We suppose that our situation is not going to improve, so what's the point? We're just one part of a never-ending cycle. We live, we die, we become fertilizer for someone else's life, who will die and become fertilizer for someone else's life, and so on. Such despair can drive us to distraction.

Egyptian monks called sloth the "noonday demon," for the heat of the sun and their growling stomachs (dinner was at 3:00 p.m.) distracted them from their spiritual duties. They fidgeted between sleep and hunger as they tried to read and pray. I would like to nominate a northern substitute for the noonday demon. Our sloth is the "six o'clock shadow," which is when the sun sets in winter and the world stretches its arms and yawns. I save tasks for after six that I can do in my sleep, because that is pretty much how I'll be doing them.

If sloth is the distraction that comes from despair, then there is no better term to describe our world. We live in the Age of Despair, when most people struggle to scratch out an existence in broken economies governed by cynical officials who often happen to possess nuclear weapons. We have little hope our lives will improve and we know that even if they do, we could all blow up if a loose nuke falls into the wrong hands.

It's no wonder that our Age of Despair drowns its sorrows in the Age of Distraction. With nothing large to live for, we fritter away our best hours online, on smart phones, or in front of a television. We surf channels and websites looking for some video or story that will divert our attention from our aimless lives. Why do we treat our phones like a third arm? Every few seconds we check for text messages. Could our need for distraction be drawn from a deeper despair? When life lacks a point we fill our lives with pointless things.

I've spoken of sloth because I suspect it lies at the root of many people's crisis of faith. More people shrug away their faith than are argued out of it. They don't have a compelling reason to stop believing in God, they just look away and say, "Meh." These doubters don't need better arguments, they need greater passion. They lack desire, not just for God but for anything of weight. Their hearts have shriveled from a sugary diet of news, sports scores, and celebrity gossip, and they don't even notice that they no longer hunger for big things. Their problem is not that they no longer believe in God. It's worse than that. They no longer even understand the question.

These malnourished people are missing out on salvation, not merely because they lack faith but also because there is not much left of them to save.* Their souls are stooped from years of scuffling beneath the low ceiling of trivialities. They don't even notice that their lives are filled with nonstop action of no importance, for their hunched hearts can't see past their feet, even when they're standing up. These cramped souls need to stretch their horizon and live for something larger than themselves, but like anything that requires effort, they can't do this on their own. They need a team of believers; they need to get to church.

The Fuel of Faith

The life of faith is a marathon, and like all races, it cannot be run alone. Hebrews follows its chapter on the heroes of faith with

---

* This is what C. S. Lewis was getting at in *The Great Divorce*. Sin dehumanizes us by ravaging our image of God within, so in a real sense we are lessened.

this encouragement: "Therefore, since we are surrounded by such a great cloud of witnesses, let us throw off everything that hinders and the sin that so easily entangles, and let us run with perseverance the race marked out for us" (12:1). We are told to "not give up meeting together, as some are in the habit of doing, but let us encourage one another—and all the more as you see the Day approaching" (10:25).

We meet together to encourage each other in the race of faith, but mostly we gather to hear the voice of God. The church is unlike any other club that we might join, for it is "God's temple," "a dwelling in which God lives by his Spirit" (1 Corinthians 3:16; Ephesians 2:19–22). Whenever the church gathers, whether large or small, God has promised to meet with us and nourish our faith by His Word and sacrament. Read Question 65 of the Heidelberg Catechism:

> *Question:* "It is by faith alone that we share in Christ and all his blessings: where then does that faith come from?"

> *Answer:* "The Holy Spirit produces it in our hearts by the preaching of the holy gospel, and confirms it through our use of the holy sacraments."

If the Holy Spirit produces faith through the proclamation of His Word, then we whose faith needs shoring up must make every effort to hear that Word. "Faith comes from hearing the message," writes Paul, "and the message is heard through the word of Christ" (Romans 10:17). Peter concurs, "For you have been born again . . . through the living and enduring word of God. . . . And this is the word that was preached to you" (1 Peter 1:23–25).

Martin Luther said that while it's important to read the Bible for ourselves, we receive special comfort when we hear that same Word expounded by another. Our eyes may read that God loves and forgives us, but we especially believe it when another person assures us it is so. Dietrich Bonhoeffer reflected on his own experience and declared, "The confidence of faith arises not only out of solitude, but also out of the assembly." There the preacher is "another who speaks, and this becomes an incomparable assurance for me."

Preaching pulls us out of the pit of doubt because it forces our knees down and our eyes up. We assume the posture of a supplicant, a hungry listener who must sit and wait for God to feed us from His Word. And since we are focused on God rather than our own doubts, we are in prime position to receive this grace from His hand.

Our faith that is born in God's Word grows strong on the sacraments of baptism and the Lord's Supper. Some Christians prefer the term "ordinance" to "sacrament," though most would agree with John Calvin's definition of a sacrament as a sign that seals our faith. Calvin said a sacrament is "an outward sign by which the Lord seals on our consciences the promises of his good will toward us in order to sustain the weakness of our faith." These physical signs make the gospel real in a uniquely powerful way, for they tangibly apply God's promise of salvation to our individual lives. It's one thing to be told that all believers have died and risen with Christ; it's a whole other experience to be that believer who is immersed and comes up dripping in the presence of God's people. It's one thing to be told that Jesus died for the sins of the world; it's quite another to hold in my hands the bread and the cup and hear that they are "The body of Christ, broken for you. The blood of Christ, shed for you."

If you are a Christian who is struggling with doubts, check whether you have been faithfully practicing the spiritual disciplines. Have you committed to a local assembly of God's people, and are you a dependable member? Have you been baptized, and do you regularly receive the Lord's Supper? The Supper is an outward sign that seals our faith, so if you feel that you are losing your faith, run to the table and hear again how much Jesus loves—not just the whole world—but directly and specifically you.

The sacraments that nourish our faith also bind us to the faithful. Baptism is a sign that unites us to the body of Christ and the Lord's Supper is called Communion because "we, who are many, are one body, for we all partake of the one loaf" (1 Corinthians 10:17). So bring the coals of your faith to church and pile them in a heap with the others. Faith that has been kindled from gathering with God's people has a good chance of staying lit when it's alone.

Come to church, and the Word that you hear and the prayers that you sing will strengthen your faith for the week.

You will still need to feed your faith on daily prayer and Bible reading, for we live in a secular, pluralistic age that often derides and dismisses our most cherished beliefs. Derision may come in your graduate program, on your lunch hour, or when you're among cynical friends who worship Jesus "ironically." You may feel your faith start to slip, and you'll need to excuse yourself, walk into a bathroom stall, close the door, and recite the Apostles' Creed you learned in church. "I believe in God, the Father almighty, creator of heaven and earth. I believe in Jesus Christ, his only Son, our Lord . . ." And you'll keep saying it until you feel again that you do believe it. Take to heart what you recite in church—memorize the Apostles' Creed and assuring passages of Scripture—for someday they may save your faith.

Are you grappling with doubts? It's not always easy to tell where they're coming from, whether from intellectual questions, boredom, or even just an interruption in your routine. C. S. Lewis candidly confessed, "I find that mere change of scene always has a tendency to decrease my faith at first—God is less credible when I pray in a hotel bedroom than when I am in College," which is where he worked. It will help to figure out why you're doubting so you can tailor a response to your specific problem. But the best help for all of them is the same: Get to church, where God's Spirit has promised to blow on the embers of your faith in the company of the faithful. You may walk away as discouraged as you went in, but I doubt it.

Chapter 13

FAITH

We cannot live without a cause, without some object of devotion, some center of worth, something on which we rely for our meaning.
H. Richard Niebuhr

Steve Jobs shifted his bony frame in the garden chair. The legendary inventor was losing his battle with pancreatic cancer, and his biographer wanted to know his thoughts on the afterlife. Jobs replied, "I'm about fifty-fifty on believing in God. For most of my life, I've felt that there must be more to our existence than meets the eye." Jobs conceded that his impending death may have inspired him to give God better odds than He deserved, but he said, "I like to think that something survives after you die. It's strange to think that you accumulate all this experience, and maybe a little wisdom, and it just goes away. So I really want to believe that something survives, that maybe your consciousness endures."

Jobs may have put the chances for God at no more than fifty-fifty, but there is no chance he lived his life without one. Skeptics sometimes say they are better off than believers because their feet are firmly planted on the ground. They haven't gone out on a limb and put their faith in a God they cannot see. But they forget that no one—not even an atheist—gets a free pass on faith. Faith is a forced choice. Everyone has some object of devotion, some being or cause that makes life worth living. Everyone invests their lives in something. This is their God.

The question that every person must answer is not "Will you believe in God?" but "Which God will you believe in?" Not "Do you have faith?" but "Where have you put your faith?" Everyone relies on some god to keep them safe and make their lives count. We all receive the same precious currency—one life—and we must choose what to spend that life on. What stock are you buying?

The only God who deserves your trust is Jesus. Paul declares, "In Christ all the fullness of the Deity lives in bodily form, and you have been given fullness in Christ" (Colossians 2:9–10). When you put your faith in Jesus, the security and significance of your life are settled. You are complete, for you are in Christ, and Christ is God. What could you ever do to top that? When you find your identity in Jesus, you won't fret about the title on your business card, the size of your home, or how many heads turn when you enter a room. It ultimately won't matter whether you write a bestseller or labor in obscurity; land a corner office or get passed over again; look half your age or old enough to be your mother. Your value is fixed and found in Jesus, and no accomplishment, or failure, can ever change that.

There are two reasons why any god other than Jesus will always let us down. First, we never serve lesser gods for their own sake, but only for the comfort and satisfaction they bring. No one trusts money, pleasure, or knowledge as ends in themselves, but only for what they do for us. But if we exploit these goods for our own benefit, then in the end we are merely serving ourselves. We are in charge. We are starring in the role of God.

This may seem wonderful, especially when we're young and invincible. Who wouldn't want to run his own life, doing whatever he wants whenever he wants just because he wants? There is just one problem, and it's big. When it comes time to die—and we all will die—we will die with whatever god we have lived for. If we have spent our lives on ourselves, then we will receive whatever help we can bring. But we are the ones who are *dying*, so we already know how that will go. Why put our trust in a god we know won't come through?

Second, the true God is a jealous God, and He doesn't usually wait for us to fall on our own. He gives us a push. He lovingly reveals the weakness of our idols by destroying us at the point of our idolatry. The gods we count on are the very things He uses to take us down.

The ancient Egyptians worshiped the Nile River and its life-giving waters, so God demonstrated His power by turning their precious river into blood. They worshiped the frog goddess who assisted in childbirth, so His next plague littered the land with leaping frogs. God's ten plagues delivered His people from Egypt, but once they settled in the Promised Land they began to hedge their bets by worshiping Baal. Baal was the Canaanite god of fertility. He was the storm god who, with lightning in one hand and thunder in the other, promised to send rain upon the Israelites' fields and make the people rich. If you are an agrarian society that lives off the land, it makes sense to diversify your deities and pray to the god of rain.

God responded by striking the Israelites at their point of compromise. You want to worship Baal for the rain he provides? Fine. Then, as Elijah told King Ahab, "As the LORD, the God of Israel, lives, whom I serve, there will be neither dew nor rain in the next few years except at my word" (1 Kings 17:1). You want to pray to the rain god? Then you will be as dry as a peanut butter and cornbread sandwich.

Twilight of the Gods

We have witnessed God's judgment in recent history. Americans entered the twentieth century with trust in *Athena*, the Greek goddess of *knowledge* and *wisdom*. We put our confidence in science, and it seemed to deliver. We discovered vaccines and surgical procedures that prolonged life, and we invented cars, airplanes, and air conditioning that made life more enjoyable than ever. But the same science that made our lives so comfortable also saddled us with nuclear weapons, greenhouse gasses, and test-tube children who have sperm donors for fathers. And just when we thought we had licked most of the garden variety diseases, we learned that our antibiotics are contributing to more virulent strains.

Athena cannot save us. Her breakthroughs solve one problem with one hand and open a new possibility for our destruction with the other. Not long ago men boarded ships and traveled great distances to fight their enemies. Now we possess the technology to destroy one another with the push of a button.

This terrified us, so in the 1960s we added *Aphrodite*, the goddess of *pleasure* and *beauty*, to our pantheon of gods. Maybe free love, unleashed from the conventions of our Victorian past, could save us. But many Americans soon discovered that sex and drugs were not the saviors they were looking for. What has the sexual revolution brought us? Venereal disease, AIDS, divorce, pornography, sexting, and shattered lives looking for someone, anyone, who will love them. Aphrodite is a terrific flirt but she's a worthless god. Those people who worshiped love learned too late that their sexual partners didn't really care about them.

Perhaps science and sex are not the answers, but you can't miss with money, can you? So in the 1980s we turned to *Artemis*, the goddess of *wealth*, who promised an ever-expanding standard of living if we followed the rules of unfettered, crony capitalism. How is that working out?

Do you see a trend here? We put our trust in science; technology threatens to take us out. We aim for love; no one has felt loved less. We go for gold; we end up broke. And we have done this as a nominally Christian nation. America didn't stop worshiping Jesus, we just pushed him aside to make room for Athena, Aphrodite, and Artemis. And because Jesus is a jealous God, science, sex, and money have become the downfall of our society.

What we experienced as a culture, Steve Jobs endured in his personal life. Friends say Jobs possessed a "reality distortion field," a unique ability to believe his own version of reality. He didn't see the world as it was but as he wanted it to be. This powerful vision would inspire Apple employees to imagine magical products and meet impossible deadlines, but it also enabled Jobs to block out unpleasant facts. It took some time to convince Jobs that he was sick, and even longer to persuade him to follow his doctors' orders. He had such confidence in his creative mind that he initially tried to cure his cancer with alternative methods. "I really didn't want them to open up my body," Jobs explained, "so I tried to see if a few other things would work." He tried acupuncture, vegetarian diets, herbal remedies, hydrotherapy, and cleansing the poison from his body by venting all negative feelings. His wife and friends begged him to have the life-saving surgery but for nine months he refused. By the time Jobs agreed to have the operation, the slow-growing cancer had spread from his pancreas to his liver.

I weep for Jobs and his untimely end, and I can't help but notice that his unyielding self-reliance illustrates the problem with idolatry: He was playing the role of God. For much of his life it seemed to work. His genius dreamed of the iPod, iPhone, and iPad, and his overpowering drive pushed his staff to break new ground to make them. He became one of history's great inventors, the Thomas Edison and Henry Ford of our time. If anyone could succeed by relying on himself it was Jobs, for his mind could bend reality to his will. Until it couldn't.

As Jobs shifted his gaunt torso in the garden chair, he seemed to realize that in the end, we're left with whatever we lived for. He had invested his fifty-six years in himself, and now he was dying. His body had betrayed him; his god had let him down.

Jobs was sitting in his backyard, and the sunny afternoon had lifted his spirits enough to think about the future. He told his biographer he would like there to be an afterlife, and then he fell silent for a long time. "But on the other hand, perhaps it's like an on-off switch," he said. "*Click!* And you're gone." He paused and smiled weakly. "Maybe that's why I never liked to put on-off switches on Apple devices."

Part 2

FOLLOWING GOD

Chapter 14

TRUST

*Never be afraid to trust an unknown
future to a known God.*
CORRIE TEN BOOM

The classic illustration for faith, which I heard in multiple sermons as a child, is about a nineteenth-century daredevil who walked a tightrope over Niagara Gorge, just below the Falls. The Great Blondin reportedly made the trip several times, with varying degrees of difficulty. He walked blindfolded, on stilts, and with his manager on his back, and once he stopped in the middle and cooked an omelet. The version I heard said that Blondin grabbed a wheelbarrow and asked a man if he believed he could push it across. When the man said yes, Blondin replied, "Then get in the wheelbarrow."

This story portrays both the confidence and uncertainty that come with faith: Confidence, because believers put their trust in what they know, and uncertainty, because they can't experience how it all turns out until it does. If faith means to commit to what we know, then faith contains both the assurance of knowledge and the risk of commitment. We may be certain of the Great Blondin's ability, but we don't have faith until we climb into his wheelbarrow. And from the other side, we won't get in unless we're sure we can trust him to carry us.

Faith includes both assurance and risk, and we are continually tempted to cheat one for the other. The next chapter explains our problems with assurance, while this one examines our feeble attempts to manage risk. Like a young Casanova who prefers to play the field rather than tie himself down to any one girl, we have commitment issues when it comes to God. We would like to remove every speck of risk from our relationship, because what if He turns out to be not exactly what we were looking for? As we will learn, our attempt to eliminate risk only generates more of it, until it ultimately ruins our faith.

Backup Plan

I thought of the Great Blondin when I watched the television special of Nik Wallenda walking a tightrope over Niagara Falls. This was a sermon illustration come to life, and promised to be the go-to illustration of faith for the next generation of preachers. I caught Wallenda's attempt when he was halfway across, and I noticed there was a cable coming from his waist to a pulley rolling behind him. I asked my family what it was, and they said it was a tether, a safety wire that would catch Wallenda in case he fell. Wallenda didn't want the tether, but the network that broadcast his feat insisted he wear it. I'm glad they did, because I didn't want to see him slip and plummet to his death.

All the same, you can't have it both ways, and Wallenda's tether made his exploit something less than death defying. Wallenda seemed to realize this. In his celebratory interview he said, "I had a tether but I didn't use it." Actually he did, for the tether provided valuable insurance. It supplied confidence as he walked through the swirling mist. Would he have been as sure-footed if he knew that one false step or gust of wind could sweep him to his death?

Wallenda was wise to have a backup plan, but what guaranteed his physical safety is the surest path to our spiritual death. The Israelites had a tether. They worshiped Yahweh, but they also hedged their bets by praying to Baal. They assumed that the God who delivered them from Egypt would continue to provide, but they figured it didn't hurt to have a plan B.

Poor Gideon didn't understand why the Israelites were starving. "If the Lord is with us," he asked the angel of the Lord, "why has all this happened to us?" (Judges 6:13). The angel told Gideon to cut the tether. He must destroy his father's altar to Baal and gather an army to fight the Midianites (vv. 14, 25). And to make sure he got the point, God whittled Gideon's army down to three hundred men (7:7).

Sometimes the very thing God uses to bless us becomes a tether. The Israelites begged Moses to pray for them when they were bitten by poisonous snakes. God answered by telling Moses to "Make a snake and put it up on a pole; anyone who is bitten can look at it and live" (Numbers 21:8). The Israelites were so thankful for the bronze snake that they kept it around, and eventually they began to ask from it what only God could provide. When King Hezekiah decided to destroy the idols in Israel, one of the things that had to go was the snake. Hezekiah "broke into pieces the bronze snake Moses had made, for up to that time the Israelites had been burning incense to it" (2 Kings 18:4).

It's easy to see how the blessing of God can become an idolatrous backup plan. We eagerly depend on God when we have nothing because we have no other options. Either God comes through for us or we're sunk. When God answers our prayer with a just-in-the-nick-of-time job, friend, or pregnancy, we learn that we can trust Him the next time we're in a pinch. We'd better learn this well, for next time it will be harder.

God's answer to prayer may have blessed us with money, connections, or a child. We now have something to lose, so the stakes are higher the next time we're in need. It's difficult to surrender everything to God when we actually have something He might take. Our swelling bank account or circle of friends provide options. We may go through the motions of telling God about our need, but our prayer isn't as desperate because we have one or two fallback plans. We would be happy for God to deliver us again, but if not, we're pretty sure we've got this. It's hard to pray from the heart, "Give us this day our daily bread," when we know our freezer is already full.

The Subtlety of Idolatry

Tim Keller says an idol is "anything more important to you than God, anything that absorbs your heart and imagination more than God, anything you seek to give you what only God can give. . . . An idol is whatever you look at and say, in your heart of hearts, 'If I have that, then I'll feel my life has meaning, then I'll know I have value, then I'll feel significant and secure.'"

Idolatry is often obvious. The businessman who repeatedly skips church and family events because he's working weekends might as well get a heart tattoo with his company logo inside. During the training week for store managers of a national chain, the CEO urged the applicants "to drink the Kool-Aid" and put the company above their own families. "We will be your family," the man said, "and we will make you successful beyond your wildest dreams." During the question and answer period my friend asked how many executives on the platform had been divorced. Every hand went up. He asked how many had been divorced twice. Every hand went up again. Then the human resources person swooped in and snatched away his microphone.

Idolatry isn't always this brazen. Sometimes it's so subtle that you'll miss it unless you know exactly what you're looking for. Many successful businessmen are also faithful Christians. They are church elders and devoted fathers, but their confidence lies more in their careers and investment portfolios than in God. If God stopped answering prayer, they might go several months before noticing. Their lives have so much momentum they could continue to chug along long after God has left them.

Good jobs and savings accounts are God's gifts to us, and all things considered I'd rather have them than do without. But these blessings can become backup plans, golden tethers that bind our hearts from following God. How can we know for sure that our faith is in God and not any possession or friend we might have?

There is only one way, and that's to share it. We clutch and cling when we're not sure God will provide what we need. We fear we're on our own, so we determine to take matters into our own hands. But when we believe that our lives are in God's hands, that God has our best interest at heart and will not let us down, then we are free to release our grip and open our hands to others.

The old hymn has it right: "Trust and obey, for there's no other way to be happy in Jesus, but to trust and obey." Trust is the key to following God, for we only give ourselves to people we think we can trust. Eve learned this lesson in Eden. Surrounded by unmistakable evidence of the goodness of God, she still succumbed to the serpent's insinuation that God wasn't on her side. "You will not surely die," the serpent said. "For God knows that when you eat of it your eyes will be opened, and you will be like God" (Genesis 3:4–5). Well, if God was against her, then she must rely on herself, and Eve ate the fruit in history's first (and failed) attempt at self-actualization.

I understand the importance of trust when I consider my own children. We have some basic rules in our house: no screaming, no writing on the walls, and pants must be worn at all times. When my children were small they thought these rules were terribly restrictive. My wife and I couldn't explain to their little minds that these rules were for their good; they just had to trust us. Now they're old enough to understand, and they're thankful to live quietly in a clean house. But there is a new set of rules involving media time, cell phones, and sleepovers that they need to trust us for now.

Every act of willing obedience comes down to trust. When my children believe our rules are for their good, they cheerfully strive to keep them. When I believe that God is for me, I enthusiastically want to do what He says. Even when it's hard. Consider Jesus' ultimatum: "If anyone would come after me, he must deny himself and take up his cross and follow me. For whoever wants to save his life will lose it, but whoever loses his life for me will find it. What good will it be for a man if he gains the whole world, yet forfeits his soul?" (Matthew 16:24–26).

I gulp every time I read this, for I wonder whether I have fully released my life to Christ or am holding something back. I want to give Jesus everything, but I often catch myself spreading the risk around. It seems foolish to put all my eggs in one basket—even if the label reads "God"—so I scatter my confidence among reliable friends, a dependable job, and a gradually growing retirement account. I essentially create a hedge fund in case Jesus' stock starts to fall. If Jesus doesn't hold up His end of our covenant, I'll find a way to muddle through, at least for a while.

My attempt to manage risk is the riskiest move I could make, for someday I'll stand alone before God. No amount of money, no title on my resume, no friend or family will make any difference then. The only questions that will matter are, Have I put all my faith in Jesus, and did I trust Him enough to gladly give my life away? If these questions trouble you as much as they bother me, there is something you can do to make sure your trust is in Jesus alone. Ask what you would rely on if Jesus does not come through for you. Where would you turn? Then tear up that plan. Enjoy your job, family, and friends as good gifts from God, just know you can't ask them to supply what only God can provide.

Many of us fight to fully commit to a God we cannot see. We instinctively want to manage risk, and so we shortchange the wholehearted reliance that God requires. There is an opposite, more spiritual way to ruin faith. This path destroys faith not by eliminating risk but by elevating it, and it's the subject of our next chapter.

Chapter 15

JUMP

When you . . . step into the darkness of the unknown,
faith is knowing that one of two things shall happen:
either you will be given something solid to stand on,
or you will be taught how to fly.
EDWARD TELLER

The opening volley in the Battle for Earth was fired in the craggy wilderness of Judea. There God challenged Satan for the championship of the world, literally. Ordinarily this would be no contest, but given what Satan had captured in their previous skirmish in Eden, God could defeat him only by becoming a man, susceptible to his arrows. Jesus must be tempted by the devil to prove He was the last Adam, the true Israelite, who had come to retrace and replace the sins of His ancestors.

God's people had deserted their faith in the desert, so God's Son went there to win it back. The first Adam sinned inside Eden and was expelled into the wilderness; the last Adam went out into the wasteland to defeat sin and lead His people back to paradise. The first Adam caved to a sin that was easily avoidable—enjoy the fruit of every tree except one; the last Adam renounced a sin that caused His body to tremble with desire—after forty days without food, how about a little bread? Adam and Eve lost their lives when they ate a fruit they thought would make them like God. Jesus, who is God, retained His deity when he refused to eat what was supposed to keep Him alive.

Satan's first two temptations were straightforward, secular attempts to talk Jesus into using a backup plan. "Sure, you could rely on God for food and the completion of your mission, or you could take matters into your own hands by turning these stones into bread and bowing before me. I'll give you the world for a song. Tip your hat in appreciation, and it's yours." Jesus was too devout to fall for these obvious sins, and He replied, "It is written: 'Worship the Lord your God and serve him only'" (Luke 4:8).

Satan had time for one more play, and he called a Hail Mary. *Okay, you're too spiritual to fall for the obvious temptations, so I'll craft a sin out of your piety. You'll never see it coming.* And so from the desert Satan brought Jesus to the holiest place on Earth, the temple in Jerusalem, where, in keeping with the mood of the place, he quoted Scripture.

"If you are the Son of God," Satan said, "throw yourself down from here. For it is written: 'He will command his angels concerning you to guard you carefully; they will lift you up in their hands, so that you will not strike your foot against a stone'" (Luke 4:9–11).

Notice the subtlety of this temptation. Satan is the one speaking, so that's a giveaway, but how many of us would have realized we were being tempted? Satan's challenge seemed spiritual, even necessary. "Do you trust your Father's promise to protect you? Then jump off this temple. Take a big risk, and see if He doesn't rush in to rescue you. If you can't rely on Him here, on the very spot where He dwells, then where can you? C'mon, Mr. Son of God, show us what you believe."

Put yourself in Jesus' sandals. Wouldn't you feel obligated to jump? "Why, I'll show you, Satan. I do believe in God. He'll catch me, I know He will. Geronimo!" And off we'd go. Before I explain why Jesus didn't jump, we need to understand why this leap of faith strikes many Christians as a good idea.

Living on a Prayer

In chapter 4 we learned that our secular, pluralistic culture assumes that faith is a blind leap because God is unknowable. Elizabeth Gilbert captures the modern mood when she writes that faith in God requires "a mighty jump from the rational over to the unknowable. . . . Faith is walking face-first and full-speed into the dark." Chapter 4 showed that when it comes to believing in God, many Christians agree with Gilbert's assumption that the uncertainty of ignorance is essential for faith. They claim that nothing kills faith faster than knowledge, and we don't have faith unless we doubt.

I agree that some uncertainty accompanies any act of faith, but it's the risk of commitment rather than the risk of doubt. We take a chance anytime we trust ourselves to something, but we reduce this risk when we commit to what we know. Not satisfied with the risk of commitment, the popular view says that our knowledge must also be uncertain, that we don't have faith unless there is uncertainty all the way down. Faith no longer means relying on what you know but rolling the dice on what you don't.

Part 1 corrected this false view of faith for *believing in God*, and now part 2 will do the same for *following God*. Many Christians surmise that if uncertainty is necessary for faith, then the higher our uncertainty the greater our faith. So faith means taking large risks. We flex our faith muscles when we attempt something so hard that we will certainly fail unless God steps in and rescues us.

One author says, "When God invites you to join Him in His work, He presents a God-sized assignment for you to accomplish. You will realize that you cannot accomplish it on your own. If God does not help you, you will fail." He is so convinced of this that he adds, "I have come to the place in my life that, if the assignment I sense God is giving me is something that I know I can handle, I know it probably is *not* from God" (emphasis his).

My college president used to say, "If you can explain it, then God didn't do it." He meant that God should get the credit for our new library, athletic center, and the godly enthusiasm that lifted our campus. He also meant to inspire us to stride confidently into our careers and, as William Carey exhorted timid pastors, "Expect great things from God" and "Attempt great things for God."

These words remind me that I have a big God who is capable of big things, and I should ask Him to bless me in big ways. I pray for my family to prosper, my church and school to grow, and my speaking and writing ministry to reach more and more people. If you are reading this, you are an answer to prayer! All things being equal, more influence is better than less.

But while we should ask for God's blessing and try new things, we should not presume that God will give us success with whatever we try. It's fine to drive to the state capitol to see if we can share our faith with the governor, but it's dangerous to say we're "challenging God's power" when we do it. It's good to join a summer missionary team in Trinidad, but it's a bit presumptuous to claim we're "taking over the island for God."

God has promised to meet our needs, so we should cry out for help when we have them. I love to hear stories of God providing for His children in spectacular ways. I am inspired when I hear of armed thugs who were scared away by angels guarding the door; a truck carrying huddled refugees that hummed for hundreds of miles on an empty tank, only to sputter and die the moment it arrived in the safety of a UN camp; a freckled teenager who knocked on the door with a stringer of speckled trout, unaware that the family inside was asking God for its dinner tonight.

We should cry out to God when we're in trouble, but it isn't faith to intentionally get ourselves in trouble and count on God to bail us out. Is it really faith for a church to operate on a "faith budget" that is 65 percent higher than it can afford? Is it faith to quit your job and move your family to Togo, not knowing how you will provide for them once you get there? Is it faith to take on debt you can't humanly pay back, or would real faith pay cash?

Many Christians think that overextending themselves is the surest path to a higher life. One author asks, "When was the last time God worked through you in such a way that you knew beyond doubt that God had done it? In fact, when was the last time you saw miracles happen on a regular basis in *your* life?" (emphasis his). He adds, "It's a frightening and utterly exhilarating truth, isn't it? As God's chosen, blessed sons and daughters, we are expected to attempt something large enough that failure is guaranteed . . . unless God steps in."

Look at that last sentence again. Where have you seen it before? It's almost exactly what Satan said to Jesus: "If you are the Son of God, then jump off this temple. Failure is guaranteed, unless God steps in." Could it be that what passes for great faith today is nothing more than the last temptation of Christ?

Trusting or Testing God?

If this discussion seems confusing, here is an easy way to distinguish genuine faith from its fakes. Faith means to commit to what we know, so we have faith when we trust God for whatever He has promised or commanded us. If we don't have a word from the Lord, then we must temper our claims to faith. We're not champions of faith when we claim a promise or obey a command that isn't there. We may just be foolish.

Faith starts *from assurance* and proceeds *to risk*. We enthusiastically take the chance of commitment when we are certain we have a word from the Lord. Counterfeit faith starts *from uncertainty* and leaps *for assurance*. We have doubts about God and our relationship with Him, so we take a huge risk and pray He will come through for us. If He saves us with an extraordinary miracle—something only He can do—then we will know for sure that we are His children and He is worthy of our trust. Our faith will be confirmed, but by putting God on trial. So we haven't trusted God, we've tested Him.

This is why Jesus refused to jump. He remembered Israel's failure in the desert, the very sin He had come to replace. He remembered that they had demanded visible signs to prove God was with them, and that Moses had warned them to "not test the LORD your God" (Deuteronomy 6:16). Jesus told Satan He would not test God, for He already knew He could trust His Father. He would show this faith when He obeyed His Father's command to go to the cross, clinging to His promise that He would rise again. Jesus didn't need to force the issue, prematurely testing His Father's strength and love. He had too much faith to jump.

The life of faith is both less and more remarkable than many Christians know. It's less because the Christian life has never been about jumping off temples but about the daily grind of obedience. It's more because anyone can hop a plane to Trinidad, drive to the state capitol, or spend money they don't have. But to love your neighbor day after day after ordinary day—that requires an act of God.

Do you want to know whether you have faith? Rest in the promises of God, obey His commands, and then do whatever comes before you (Colossians 3:17, 23–24). Do it over and over again and you'll leave a legacy of faith, a life that pleases God.

Chapter 16

FAITHFULNESS

The world has yet to see what God can do
with a man fully consecrated to him.
DWIGHT L. MOODY

A bright beep sounded in my ear. I guessed that meant it was my turn so I asked, "Hello?" The voice on the other end said, "You're on with Lee Hamilton, Sports Talk 640. What's on your mind?" I wanted to die, or at least hang up.

The day before Nolan Ryan had pitched a no-hitter through the first seven innings of Monday Night Baseball. I was only eleven or twelve, but since it was summer my parents let me stay up. During the eighth inning a batter blooped a Ryan fastball into shallow right field. The outfielder dashed in and dove for the ball but couldn't quite reach it. The ball bounced in front of his glove for a single, or what would have been a single if the official scorer, sympathetic to Ryan's cause, hadn't decided it was an error. The questionable scoring became moot when a later batter hit a ball that landed too far from a fielder to charge with an error, and Ryan had to settle for a one-hitter.

This was June in northeast Ohio, and since the hometown Cleveland Indians were already out of the pennant race and Lee Hamilton had three hours of sports talk to fill, he spent the afternoon ranting about the error that should have been a base hit. Like many radio personalities, Hamilton was prone to exaggeration. At one point he said that it was wrong to charge the right fielder with an error because even God couldn't have caught that ball.

His words pierced my childlike faith and pricked my conscience. Instantly I knew what I had to do. I had to call his show and take a stand for God. I was terrified. I had never called a talk show before, and I haven't since. I told myself I was just a kid; no one would care about my opinion. What if Hamilton mocked me like he sometimes did other callers with whom he disagreed? He might tell the world I was a religious freak, or worse.

All true, but I couldn't shake the compulsion that I must defend God's honor. I *needed* to make this call. After a half hour of dithering I finally wrestled my fears to the ground, picked up the phone, and quickly dialed the number. I was sorry to get through, and surprised to hear my voice telling the screener I had a comment about the Nolan Ryan game. I couldn't back out now.

The screener put me on hold, and I listened to the show through my telephone until a beep suddenly sounded in my earpiece. I took a deep breath and said I agreed with Mr. Hamilton that the right fielder had no chance to catch the ball and should not have been charged with an error. "And one other thing," I said. "You mentioned that not even God could have caught that ball. I think that's wrong. God would have made the catch." Lee Hamilton must have pegged my voice for the child that I was. He thanked me for calling, agreed that God would surely catch any ball hit His way, and promised to be more careful in the future.

A wave of euphoria washed over my head and down to my toes when I hung up the phone. I wasn't happy, just relieved. Very, very relieved. I had heard the call of God and I had answered it. At least that's what I believed.

Trying Faith

Years later I wonder whether that childhood phone call was an expression of faith. Faith means to commit to what I know, so the important question is how did I know God wanted me to call the show? No Scripture verse commands me to phone every talk show that dishonors the name of God, and that's a good thing. Most of my life would be spent on hold, waiting for my chance to stick up for God. Now that I'm older I also realize that Lee Hamilton's remark wasn't necessarily an attack on God. Hamilton was exaggerating for effect, but my overly literal mind didn't yet grasp hyperbole. I don't think he meant to harm the name of God, and I doubt that God took much offense.

But is it still possible that God was nudging me to call? Many Christians believe that God communicates His will to them outside the pages of Scripture. One author says that besides the Bible, God tells us what He wants us to do through prayer, circumstances, and the church. There is no formula or method for discerning when God is speaking, but if we cultivate a close relationship with God, we will know when it happens.

This leader raises the stakes when he writes, "If you have trouble hearing God speak, you are in trouble at the very heart of your Christian experience."

On the other hand he warns, "You also need to be very careful about claiming you have a word from God. Claiming to have a word from God is serious business. . . . If you have not been given a word from God yet you say you have, you stand in judgment as a false prophet." So you must "be very careful how you interpret circumstances. Many times we jump to a conclusion too quickly."

On the other, previous hand, he cautions that we shouldn't be too slow in claiming a word from the Lord, for "The moment God speaks to you is the very moment God wants you to respond."

Yikes! This back-and-forth advice is bound to burden many Christians with false guilt. It doesn't seem fair to tell people they must hear God's voice or their relationship is in trouble, and then inform them that there is no formula so they'll have to figure it out on their own. If you are trapped in this spiral of guilt, ask yourself if your loving Father would hold you accountable for following a command you aren't sure is from Him. And if it isn't in the Bible, how would you know for sure?

God may speak outside the pages of Scripture, because God can speak whenever and wherever He wants. But we should become increasingly humble about our claims the further we get from Scripture. I know that the Bible verse I'm reading is the Word of God, but I am less sure about the conviction I feel while reading it and even less sure about my ideas for applying it. I may believe my conviction and application come from God, but I won't put them on the same plane as Scripture. So I'll temper my claims with "I think this verse means," "I sense God is leading me," or "This seems to be what God wants me to do."

I am more ambivalent about impressions or ideas that pop into my head unannounced and with no Scripture attached. God may be prompting me to start a conversation with a stranger, comment on a blog post, or buy coffee for the car behind me in the Starbucks drive-through. But I can't be sure, so I should be careful when say I know it was Him. I also must remember that Scripture is all I need to follow God, so I'm not a second-class Christian if I hear God's voice only in what He has written there. True faith trusts what we know God has revealed. We aren't responsible for not obeying what we aren't sure is from Him.*

Faith Trying

Whether or not God was compelling me to call the radio show, I believe it was an expression of faith for two reasons. First, it matters that I believed God wanted me to call. I couldn't prove that God was prompting me, but I knew I couldn't live with myself if I didn't stick up for Him. It is always wrong to violate conscience, for "everything that does not come from faith is sin" (Romans 14:23). Paul had a word from God that "no food is unclean in itself"

---

* Some readers may be troubled by John 10:27: "My sheep listen to my voice; I know them, and they follow me." Doesn't this mean that we should be able to recognize Jesus' voice whenever and wherever He speaks? In context, Jesus was speaking to unbelieving Jews who demanded an unambiguous declaration that He was the Messiah so they could attack Him. He was not referring to our ability to recognize His voice through prayer, circumstances, and other Christians. You meet the requirements of this verse if you hear His voice when you read Scripture.

(Romans 14:14). He knew that some Jewish Christians believed they should continue to keep their strict Jewish diet, and he said these sensitive souls must not be pressured to disobey their conscience. They would sin if they ate pork, not because eating pork is wrong, but simply because they thought it was.

If you are troubled by an overly sensitive conscience, try calming it with knowledge. I learned eventually that sports hyperbole should not be taken literally, and I no longer confront broadcasters who say "Brady is bigger than God" or "Tiger's return is more anticipated than the second coming."

We may educate our conscience but we must never violate it. If you remain convinced that God wants you to do something, then you must do it, even if you don't have chapter and verse. You may be mistaken, but it's dangerous to disobey what you think God is telling you. Your faith will fossilize if you repeatedly reject what you believe is from Him.

Second, my phone call was an expression of faith because it sprang from my confidence in God. Faith means to commit to *what* I know, but this relies on a deeper trust in *who* I know. I won't believe this particular promise or obey that specific command unless I trust the person who made them. And this general trust in the person will carry me even when he or she doesn't offer a specific command or promise.

My children show their faith in my wife and me when they obey our explicit commands about what to wear, when to study, and how to treat each other. We don't have commands for everything they do (some days it just seems that way to them!). Instead we want them to have as much freedom as we can trust them with. In these areas of freedom they show their faith in us by their eagerness to try new things. Child psychologist John Bowlby says life is best organized as a series of daring ventures from a secure base. When our children know they have a safe and strong home, they are liberated to launch little forays into life. They can try out for the soccer team, challenge for first chair in band, and sit by the scary kid at lunch. If they fail in any of these adventures, they know they'll always have a place in our home. That is, unless it's

2040, and then they should seriously consider finding a place of their own.

Likewise, I commit to *what* I know every time I claim a particular promise or obey an explicit command. But what about the many times I don't have a specific word from God? I can still have faith, not in a specific promise or command but in the general promise that my loving Father will never leave or forsake me (Hebrews 13:5). As Paul said, "I know whom I have believed, and am convinced that he is able to guard what I have entrusted to him for that day" (2 Timothy 1:12). Paul's faith in Jesus motivated him to make plans to visit Spain. As far as we know, Paul didn't have a promise or command from God to go to Spain, but his confidence in whom he believed inspired him to try. We don't know whether Paul ever made it to Spain, but we know he trusted enough in Jesus to take a shot.

And so it is a "step of faith" when Christians start a new ministry or business, adopt a special needs child, take a pay cut to stay in their community, send their manuscript to a publisher, walk across the room to say hello, or any number of ways we start a journey without knowing the destination or how we will get there. We may not have a specific promise to claim or command to obey, but we know Jesus, and we're willing to take a chance on Him. We can't tell how our endeavor will turn out—whether it will seem successful by those who count such things—but we know that Jesus has promised to stay with us no matter what.

How much risk we take depends a lot on how God wired us. The same freedom that empowers some to be daring permits others not to swing at every pitch. We need missionaries who boldly say they'll go to Spain, but we also need normal folks to pay to get them there. We need fearless entrepreneurs who are willing to fail until finally one start-up succeeds, but we also need ordinary people to be their customers and employees.

Most of us won't roll the dice with our life savings, but we all must learn to stretch. I have a friend who asks, "What is happening here that only God can do?" I'm tempted to talk about the new buildings on my campus or the mounting reach of my school, but even non-Christians have successful enterprises that exponentially prosper.

When seeking evidence that God is at work in your life, look for the things you can't measure. Do you forgive those you'd rather punch, remain content as you live with less, and scrape together your last shreds of hope, piling them all on God? This is proof that God is near, for unlike stories of fantastic success, these commands are actually found in Scripture! God doesn't require you to be spectacular; He does expect you to be faithful.

Chapter 17

PROMISE

*He is no fool who gives up what he cannot keep
to gain what he cannot lose.*
JIM ELLIOT

The next three chapters are dedicated to my parents, who often reminded me that "you can't learn everything in a book." I read a lot as a boy and my parents, fearing that I might be lacking in common sense, prodded me to "get your nose out of your book" and into the real world, which was often messier than what I read.

Their warning applies here. Remember our definition of faith? Faith means to commit to what we know, and that knowledge comes from God's promises and commands. So we have faith whenever we claim God's promise or obey His command. But what to do when we're not sure what God wants us to do? The next three chapters will sort through the difficult questions that befuddle Christians who desperately want to please God, if only they knew how.

My parents were right, real life often defies neat categories and you can't learn everything from a book. But some things you can, and so decades later I'm responding to their counsel with lessons from real people in the real world. And just to get even, I'm telling these stories in a book.

The Big Give

Mark hadn't slept much the night before. He served on the board of a rescue mission that needed to replace its ramshackle money pit of a building. A fund-raiser netted 30 percent of what was needed, and a foundation pledged two hundred thousand more. The mission was still short a half of a million dollars, so the board asked Mark if he would loan them the rest. He had just enough money in his retirement account, but he couldn't afford to lose it.

Mark was paralyzed by fear. On the one hand he didn't want to disappoint his friends on the board or leave an important ministry in the lurch. But he needed his life savings, and there was no guarantee that the mission would be able to repay his loan. Mark's spot on the board meant he saw the mission's books, and if present economic trends continued, there was cause for concern. His fellow board members would apologize if the mission went under or couldn't pay, but Mark would be the one in financial ruin.

After explaining the situation, Mark looked from his pastor to his coffee cup and asked for prayer. "If I had more faith, I think I could give them the loan." Pastor Joe assured him that he would pray for wisdom, and then said that faith means committing to what we know. "They're asking you to commit to uncertainty," he said. "That's not faith. It might just be foolish."

Mark's eyes widened with surprise, so Joe tried to explain why faith might decide to keep the money. "Scripture tells us to take care of our family first, so it might be a sin to risk the money that you and your wife will need to survive." Joe opened his Bible and read 1 Timothy 5:8, "If anyone does not provide for his relatives, and especially for his immediate family, he has denied the faith and is worse than an unbeliever." Joe pressed the point, "If you can no longer support your family because you've lost your retirement savings, then you've disobeyed God."

Mark knew his Bible too, and he countered with Philippians 4:19. "Doesn't the Bible promise that God will supply all of our needs?"

"Yes," Joe agreed. "But He can't supply our needs if we give away His supply."

Mark protested, "I thought we can't out-give God. Doesn't the Bible say that?"

"You're probably thinking of 2 Corinthians 9:10–11." Joe flipped a few pages. "Now he who supplies seed to the sower and bread for food will also supply and increase your store of seed and will enlarge the harvest of your righteousness. You will be made rich in every way so that you can be generous on every occasion."

Joe stopped reading. "This does seem to say that God will give back enough so we can keep giving, but I'm not sure it's a guarantee. My uncle claimed this verse when he mortgaged his house to buy his church's bonds for their building campaign. The church eventually split over their newly acquired debt and stopped making their bond payments. My uncle defaulted on his mortgage and was forced to move into a rental. Now he gets by on his pension and his kids' kindness. So while Paul's assurance is generally true, I don't think it's an ironclad promise."

After several more minutes of back and forth, Joe had an idea. "Tell you what. If faith means to commit to what we know, then you need to know whether God wants you to do this. Give me three days to look in the Bible for a promise or command that will apply to your situation, and then let's meet again."

Joe finished his research in a day and a half and cleared his schedule for lunch, where he delivered his verdict between bites of a Reuben and fries. "I began my study in 2 Corinthians 8–9, because it's the most extensive passage on giving in the Bible."

"I know, I know." Mark faked a groan. "God loves a 'hilarious' giver. It's mentioned in every sermon on stewardship. How can I forget?"

Joe smiled at his friend. "Then you'll be happy to know that the verse you're alluding to, 2 Corinthians 9:7, also says that God does not command you to give a specific amount to a specific cause. Paul says, 'Each man should give what he has decided in his heart to give, not reluctantly or under compulsion, for God loves a cheerful giver.' Bottom line is you're free to give however much you decide. Your giving should be generous but unforced. If you loan your retirement savings to the mission because you think you must, then you've missed

God's point. He leaves the size of your gift to you, so you're not disobeying if you give only a portion or none at all. It's up to you."

Joe continued, "The only command that applies to your situation is what I mentioned last time: You are responsible to God to
supply the needs of your family. So can you continue to provide for
your family if you lose this money?"

Mark nodded. "At first I didn't think so, but yesterday I ran the
numbers with Sara. We'd have to significantly downsize, but we'd
survive. So, yes, I can provide for my family without this money."

"That changes things," said Joe. "The other day I pushed back
because I was under the impression that you needed this money
to live. You still aren't obligated to give, but you're not violating a
command if you do."

"That's a relief." Mark grinned. "I'd hate to risk all this money
and find out later it was a sin!"

"I hear you," said Joe. "Okay, that does it for the commands.
Next question: Can you claim any promises in Scripture if you
loan this money? Besides the ones we've already discussed, 2 Corinthians 9:10–11 and Philippians 4:19, I've found a few others." Joe
pushed his notes across the table.

- Luke 6:38—"Give, and it will be given to you."
- Psalm 112:5—"Good will come to him who is generous and
  lends freely."
- Psalm 37:25–26—"I was young and now I am old, yet I
  have never seen the righteous forsaken or their children beg-
  ging bread. They are always generous and lend freely; their
  children will be blessed."
- Malachi 3:10—"'Bring the whole tithe into the storehouse,
  that there may be food in my house. Test me in this,' says the
  Lord Almighty, 'and see if I will not throw open the flood-
  gates of heaven and pour out so much blessing that you will
  not have room enough for it.'"

Mark put down his sandwich and sighed. "These are impressive
promises! How can I not give the money?"

"Slow down, big spender!" Joe laughed. "Remember three things. First, these are promises, not commands. They say what will happen if you give to the mission, but they don't say, or even imply, that you must. God leaves it up to you, remember?"

"Second, while these promises are generally true, they don't guarantee prosperity in every case. There are exceptions." Joe opened his Bible to Hebrews 11:37–39. "Scripture's classic chapter on faith ends with champion believers who 'went about in sheepskins and goatskins, destitute, persecuted and mistreated—the world was not worthy of them. They wandered in deserts and mountains, and in caves and holes in the ground . . . none of them received what had been promised.' Yet it wasn't as if God had failed them. God's ultimate promise—which He guarantees will come true—is the return of Jesus, the resurrection of our bodies, and the redemption of all things. It's better to give with this final promise in view rather than the certainty that God will replenish your cash in this lifetime. You could loan the money and never see a dime. It happens."

"And your last point?" asked Mark.

Joe took a sip from his glass. "My third and final point is that since this is your retirement savings, it's all the money you have to give. It's important to consider that if you say yes to the mission, you won't be able to respond to any other needs. This is your legacy gift, so make sure that the mission is where you want to invest. If you say no to the mission, you aren't saying no to God. You're just keeping your options open so you can say yes to another opportunity that comes along."

They talked awhile longer and closed their meal in prayer. The more they talked, the more it seemed that Mark would loan the mission the money, if only he could work up the courage. Joe promised to keep him in prayer and check back in a week.

Foolish Faith?

Three days later Mark called. "I want you to be the first to know that Sara and I have decided to pledge the money."

"Really? That's great!" said Joe. "What made up your mind?"

"You'll never guess," said Mark. "I was sorting through some boxes for a yard sale when I came across a plaque that used to hang in my parents' dining room. It read, 'Only one life, 'twill soon be past; Only what's done for Christ will last.' I realized that it had been easier to believe this when I was a boy and had my whole life in front of me but little to offer the Lord. Now my life is almost past, and I'm thinking that the safest thing I could do with God's money is invest it in His cause. If I believe that 'whoever sows generously will also reap generously,' then it's time to show God the money."

Joe wasn't sure the plaque was a sign from God, but he was impressed by Mark's decision to give everything. "This is the Mark I love," said Joe. "I pray that someday I'll be half as generous as you. Can I ask you one question? If you had decided not to loan the money, do you think that also would have been an expression of faith?"

Mark didn't hesitate. "No. How could that be faith? I wouldn't have been taking a chance at all then!"

Joe didn't think it was the right time to correct his friend's understanding of faith, so he congratulated him on his courage to trust God with his life savings. He asked God to bless his friend—to repay his faith with even more seed to scatter—and asked me if I would share this story with you. I changed enough of the details to mask Mark and Sara's identity, but I am challenged by their example of sacrifice.

Faith doesn't require us to foolishly put ourselves at risk, though sometimes people of faith will risk more than they otherwise would. As one who would make the ultimate sacrifice explained, "He is no fool who gives up what he cannot keep to gain what he cannot lose." Time will tell if Mark's decision was a wise investment or a waste of precious resources, but one thing is certain, Mark is no fool. His generosity will be rewarded, if not here, then in the hereafter. He gave away what he could not keep, and he will gain what he cannot lose.

Chapter 18

COMMAND

*There are no good works except those which
God has commanded, even as there is no sin
except that which God has forbidden.*
Martin Luther

Few topics are more controversial than discerning the will of God. Many Christians seek God's leading for the big decisions of life—Whom should I marry? What career should I pursue? Where should I live? Others also wait on God to tell them what car to buy, what sport to play, and which checkout line to enter. It may be comforting to think that God is dictating every decision, no matter how small, but the inevitable problem with this approach is, how do you know? How can you tell whether your impression is from God, yourself, or something you ate?

This ostensibly spiritual method might cause you to overcomplicate matters and miss God's blessing when it's staring you in the face. Recently a college student asked if I thought God had picked out one person for each of us to marry, and if so, how would he know? I asked if he was referring to Kate, a pretty, godly woman who was humble enough to date him. I appreciated that he was willing to give up his dream girl if God said no, but I told him he'd best not overthink this one. Put a ring on her finger before she realizes she could do better!

I've noticed something else. Those who claim that God directs every decision frequently find God is telling them to forsake ordinary matters for the higher, spiritual life. These are the people who switch majors from business to Bible because they think it's better to be in "full-time ministry." Why be an engineer or doctor when you can be a pastor or missionary? They skip exercise and their normal tasks to attend multiple Bible studies each week, because "physical training is of some value, but godliness has value for all things" (1 Timothy 4:8). Their house might be dustier than a Saharan camel, but you should hear them pray!

These earnest believers might be surprised to learn that both counts—receiving direct, extrabiblical commands from God and dividing the world between upper and lower stories—are out of step with the Reformation discovery of Martin Luther. This is his story.

Chapter 2 described how Luther promised to become a monk if Saint Anne would deliver him from a violent thunderstorm. Luther's impetuous vow angered his father, who had sacrificed to send Luther to law school so he could land a good job to support the family. Now, two years later, old Hans chose to take the high road and attend his son's first Mass.

It did not go well. When Luther came to the words, "We offer unto thee, the living, the true, the eternal God," he said he became "utterly stupefied and terror-stricken. I thought to myself, 'With what tongue shall I address such Majesty, seeing that all men ought to tremble in the presence of even an earthly prince?'" Luther's quivering hands nearly dropped the bread and the cup, but he steadied himself and with faltering voice managed to muddle through.

Utterly drained, he limped to his family's table where he longed to hear an encouraging word. Nothing was forthcoming, so during dinner Luther decided to force the issue. He turned to his dad and asked, "Dear father, why were you so contrary to my becoming a monk? And perhaps you are not quite satisfied even now. The life is so quiet and godly."

This was more than Hans could take and he blew up in front of the invited guests. "You learned scholar," he seethed, "have you never read in the Bible that you should honor your father and your mother? And here you have left me and your dear mother to look after ourselves in our old age."

Luther was prepared for his father's attack. He answered that being a monk was helping the family, for his prayers would do more good than money ever could. Besides, he had no choice in the matter—God had called him from the storm.

Hans replied, "God grant it was not an apparition of the Devil."

The words plunged deep into Luther's chest. Fourteen years later, after Luther had ignited the Reformation and been evicted from the Roman Catholic Church, he wrote a letter to his father that acknowledged his words "penetrated to the depths of my soul and stayed there, as if God had spoken by your lips." Luther recalled that when he had rebuked his father for his anger, Hans "suddenly retorted with a reply so fitting and so much to the point that I have hardly ever in all my life heard any man say anything which struck me so forcibly and stayed with me so long. 'Have you not also heard,' you said, 'that parents are to be obeyed?'"

Luther now conceded his father was right. He had violated God's command to obey his parents, so how could it have been God's will for him to enter the monastery? The quiet life of prayer and fasting seemed spiritual, but he had no command from God to withdraw from the world into the cloister. Luther had forsaken life's "lesser" duties—which God had clearly commanded—to pursue the "higher" life of monastic devotion—which Scripture says nothing about. And so Luther concluded that his monastic life, though overtly and incessantly spiritual, had been nothing but sin.

Lessons from Luther

Luther's story conveys two points on discerning God's will. First, it's important that God's command to obey our parents comes from Scripture. If faith means to trust God's promise or obey God's command, then the believer must know that the promise or command is from God. And unless it's found in Scripture, how would you know that?

Luther had little patience with the "spiritualists" and "enthusiasts" who claimed to receive direct revelations from God. He feared their new revelations would diminish their reliance on Scripture and open the door to strange ideas. They could say just about anything, and as long as it didn't contradict Scripture, who could say they were wrong? Luther said he would not listen to them even if they "had swallowed the Holy Ghost, feathers and all."

Luther thought their extrabiblical revelations were no more reliable than Roman Catholicism's extrabiblical traditions. He replied that Scripture has such authority "that we are under no obligation to accept anything the Bible does not assert. . . . But concerning anything not found in Scripture you should say . . . : 'When did God ever make that statement?'"

Such uncertainty is a problem for monks, who never know whether their human traditions are pleasing to God. Luther explained:

> Not one of them can say: God has commanded me to celebrate Mass, to sing matins, to observe the seven daily hours of prayer, and the like; for Scripture does not contain one word on the subject. Therefore if they are asked whether they are confident and assured that their state pleases God, they say no. But if you ask an insignificant maidservant why she scours a dish or milks the cow, she can say: "I know that the thing I do pleases God, for I have God's Word and commandment . . ." God does not look at the insignificance of the acts but at the heart that serves Him in such little things.

Luther's distinction between the spiritual elites and the "insignificant maidservant" brings us to our second point: limiting our duties to the commands of Scripture opens vast space for Christian freedom. In his *Treatise on Good Works*, Luther said that the first commandment to have no other gods frees the Christian to do anything—however small and insignificant—that steers clear of that.

The first commandment unlocks the door to Christian freedom, for our faith in Jesus aims even common activities for His glory and receives His forgiveness whenever we fall short. God declares us to be righteous in His Son, and since we cannot do anything to add to or subtract from this righteousness, we are free to do any good thing we want. We don't need to strive for heroic feats of piety. If our heart is "confident that it pleases God, then the work is good, even if it were so small a thing as picking up a straw." But "if the confidence is not there, or if he has any doubt about it, then the work is not good, even if the work were to raise all the dead and if the man were to give his body to be burned." Luther explained in another sermon:

> All the world talks about doing good. But do you want to know how you are to do good? Listen. Do not act the part of those fools who examine the various works and undertake to select such as are good and to reject such as are bad, thereby making a distinction between the works as such. No, not so! Leave the works in one class. Consider one as good as another. Fear God, and be just, as has been said. And then do whatever comes before you. This way all will be well done even though it is no more than loading manure or driving a mule.

Luther's point is that God cares far less about what we do than the spirit in which we do it. No act is too small to receive His reward, if done from faith and devotion to Him. And no act is too great to receive His judgment, if done from selfishness and pride. Do you want to please God? Keep the first commandment, "then do whatever comes before you."

An important aside: Luther observed that the first commandment is "the commandment to believe," for God is ordering us to put all of our "confidence, trust, and faith in [Him] alone and in no one else." This command carried Luther through his dark night of the soul and enabled him to counsel others. He reminded doubters that God has commanded them to hope and believe, so their doubts are a form of disobedience. If for no other reason, they must believe in God because He has commanded them. If they still find it hard to believe, they should not despair over their doubts but instead should "humble [themselves] before God, deploring this fact, and in this way begin with a weak spark of faith and strengthen it more and more every day by exercising it in all [their] living and doing."

The Will of God

How should we go about discerning God's will? By limiting ourselves to what we find in Scripture, which means focusing on God's moral will. For instance, Scripture does not tell Christians who to marry or what career to pursue. It tells us who not to marry (unbelievers—2 Corinthians 6:14) and what jobs not to take (evil ones—1 Corinthians 10:31), but it allows us to choose among the remaining options.

"It is God's will," wrote Paul, "that you should be sanctified" (1 Thessalonians 4:3). This doesn't involve marrying the "right" person or finding the "right" career, but it means guarding our sexual purity (vv. 3–8), loving our brothers and sisters (vv. 9–10), and quietly working to supply our own needs (vv. 11–12). This is God's will, whether we're married or whatever job we have.

God is more interested in *how* we live than *what* we do for a living, *where* we live, and *who* we live with. You are free to choose any number of wholesome careers, but having chosen one you must follow Scripture's command to "work at it with all your heart, as working for the Lord" (Colossians 3:23). You are free to marry any Christian single, but having chosen one, you must "become one flesh" in an inviolable bond of love and submission (Ephesians 5:21–33). You are free to live anywhere you please, but having chosen a locale you must "seek the peace and prosperity of the city" (Jeremiah 29:7).

This doesn't mean that Scripture has nothing to say about the what, where, and who questions. When faced with a difficult decision, list the central values of Scripture and then rank them according to your lot in life. For example, Scripture teaches us to value our spouses and children, but this would have little impact on a

single person's decision to relocate. Scripture commands us to provide for our aging parents and grandparents (1 Timothy 5:4), but
this would not influence the decision of someone whose parents are
self-reliant or deceased.

Once you have ranked your biblical values, prayerfully consider
which option best fits the highest ones. If more than one option
seems acceptable, ask God for wisdom and take your choice. You
have just stepped out in faith, for you have conformed your decision
to the values and commands of Scripture.

Some decisions are excruciatingly difficult. When overwhelmed
by the choices before you, remember that you will choose something. Even the decision not to choose is a vote for the status quo.
Also remember that, with the notable exception of marriage, most
decisions are not permanent. Life changes may rearrange our rank-
ing of values, forcing us to revisit earlier commitments and forge
new pathways of faith. We'll examine that scenario next.

Chapter 19

CALL

*God calls us to himself so decisively that everything
we are, everything we do, and everything we have is
invested with a special devotion and dynamism lived
out as a response to his summons and service.*

OS GUINNESS

The signs were sporadic, like an occasional wave that trickled further inland than the others, but eventually the erosion of Muriel's mind was too obvious to ignore. She repeated the same story to the same people, forgot to serve dessert when she hosted a dinner, jumbled the lines of the script on her radio show, and stumbled over Bible passages she once knew by heart. Still, her diagnosis of early onset Alzheimer's shocked her husband, Robertson McQuilkin, who was in his fifties and president of Columbia Bible College.

Robertson knew that Muriel's deteriorating condition would eventually require round-the-clock care. Should he retire from his flourishing ministry to provide that care, or should he put Muriel in a nursing home and carry on with God's business? Trusted friends urged the latter, reminding him that we must "hate" our wives for the sake of Jesus and His kingdom (Luke 14:26). Besides, Muriel would adjust to her new environment, and her slipping mind would soon enough not even know what she was missing.

Robertson wouldn't have it. Forty-two years ago he had vowed to stand by his wife, "in sickness and in health . . . till death do us part," and he wasn't about to back out now. Muriel had given him the best years of her life, and he was honored to return the favor. "There are others who can lead the Bible college," he said, "but I am the only one who can care for Muriel."

And care for her he did. It's hard to imagine a more powerful love than the devotion Robertson and Muriel shared in the last decade of her life. Initially Robertson hired a companion to stay with Muriel while he went to work, but soon Muriel would become alarmed and follow him. Sometimes at night, when he helped her undress for bed, he would find her feet bloodied from miles of speed walking trips to the college. Robertson was overwhelmed by her desire to be with him, and realized, "With me, she was content; without me, she was distressed, sometimes terror stricken."

Robertson decided to resign to focus his attention on Muriel, even though he knew he could never fully calm her dimming mind. He received less of her now, even as he gave more. He bathed her, fed her for two hours at a time, and learned to change diapers. All the while she lost more of her faculties—her speech, her legs, and finally her arms went limp.

Well-meaning friends encouraged Robertson to pay someone else to do this job and get back to serving God. One wrote, "Muriel doesn't know you anymore, doesn't know anything, really, so it's time to put her in a nursing home and get on with life." Robertson replied, "That day may come—when, because of a change in my health or hers, she could be better cared for by others—but for now, she needs me, and I need her."

The last phrase to leave Muriel's vocabulary was "I love you." She said it often to Robertson, until even that was swept away by the pounding surf of her disease. Valentine's Day was particularly poignant, because that was the day Robertson proposed to Muriel in 1948. Now, nearly a half century later, he kissed Muriel good night on Valentine's Eve and whispered a prayer: "Dear Jesus, you love sweet Muriel more than I, so please keep my beloved through the night; may she hear the angel choirs."

The next morning he was peddling his exercise bike at the foot of their bed when Muriel awoke, smiled, and spoke for the first time in months, "Love . . . love . . . love." Robertson ran to her side and wrapped his arms around her. "Honey, you really do love me, don't you?" Muriel held him with her eyes and said, "I'm nice," which was her way of saying yes. Those were the last words she ever spoke.

Every Call Counts

Muriel survived another eight years under the tender love of her devoted husband. Robertson never regretted caring for his wife, though he did wonder why God had put him on the shelf. Once a student asked if he missed being president of Columbia Bible College. Robertson replied that he hadn't thought about it, and he enjoyed his new duties of cooking and cleaning for Muriel. But that night in bed Robertson tossed as he turned the student's question over in his mind. He told God he was happy in his current role, "But if a coach puts a man on the bench, he must not want him in the game. You needn't tell me, of course, but I'd like to know—why didn't you need me in the game?"

Muriel was still mobile at this time, and the next morning she and Robertson shuffled around their block, holding hands as they went. A drunken man staggered past them, looked back, and said, "Tha's good. I likes 'at. Tha's real good. I likes it." He turned and headed down the street, mumbling to himself, "Tha's good. I likes it."

Robertson felt this unlikely source was delivering a message from the Lord. He squeezed Muriel's hand and prayed, "It is you who are whispering to my spirit, 'I likes it, tha's good.' I may be on the bench, but if you like it and say it's good, that's all that counts."

Whether or not the drunk was channeling a word from God, Robertson's theological instincts were exactly right. He embraced Luther's insight that we are free in Christ to do every calling, no matter how small, for the Lord. When friends encouraged him to remain president because serving God is more important than family, Robertson replied, "To put God first means that all other responsibilities are first, too." He served God when he was a college president and he served God just as much, if not more, as Muriel's husband. Robertson may have thought he was on the bench, but he was never more in the game. His decision to resign and care for Muriel inspired pastors to share their story and couples to renew their marriage vows. Years later when a Christian leader announced that Alzheimer's disease is a kind of death that justifies divorce, he was silenced with the story of Robertson and Muriel. After their example of selfless devotion, how could anyone think it's permissible to leave a marriage that is no longer working for them?

Answer Your Call

Robertson knew he was called to serve Muriel, but how can *you* tell what God has called *you* to do? Our primary call is to follow Jesus, but the shape of that call looks different for each of us, depending on our lot in life. To discover your divine callings, start with the people you are in covenant with. If you are married, that would be your spouse and the children who are the fruit of your covenant. Your list should also include your parents, as you are the fruit of their union, which God intended to occur within the covenant of marriage. Perhaps surprisingly, it should also include the members of your church. The largest reason to join a church is to enter into covenant fellowship with believers who are joined to Christ. We are accountable to them and they to us, and we have more say in each other's lives than most of us know or use.

Here is how this looks in my life: I answer the call of Jesus by being a Christian, husband, father, son, brother, and active member of the body of Christ. These are all ways I express my devotion to Jesus, and when I joyfully perform these callings I serve my Lord who saved me. These are my highest callings, and they are too important to be paid. I would be insulted if my wife said, "Thank you for being my husband, here's twenty dollars." Or if my child said, "You've been a good dad this week. Keep my allowance."

This will be important to remember should you ever lose your job. You may have temporarily lost the calling you are paid to perform, but your most significant callings remain unchanged. You are always called to follow Jesus, no matter what, and you are always called to serve your immediate family and your brothers and sisters in your local church. These callings stay the same, even during hard times. When your legs have been kicked out from under you and you're desperately looking for work, that is the time you most need to stay connected and committed to your covenant people.

Your covenant relationships still leave room for other callings, both paid and unpaid. How to decide what God is calling you to do, either as a paid job or in your free time? Ask yourself three questions: What do I enjoy? What do I do well? And what does the world need? Find where the answers intersect and you will find God's call, for in His providence He has formed and equipped you to meet a specific need in His world. Frederick Buechner explains, "The place God calls you to is the place where your deep gladness and the world's deep hunger meet."

Your gladness and the world's hunger both count. You may enjoy stamp collecting, but this doesn't seem to fill a void in the world. The world may not need more stamp collectors. Thanks to digital communication, soon it might not even need stamps! That's okay. You can still collect stamps as a hobby, or *avocation*, and perhaps use the skills or knowledge you honed there in a *vocation*, or calling the world needs—say museum curator or history teacher.

Working the problem from the other direction, the world needs doctors, but if you find more joy in caring for animals, then it's okay to become a veterinarian. We need vets too. The world needs pastors, but if you enjoy geometric problems and working with your hands, it's okay to become a plumber. Even pastors need plumbers. When contemplating a career, you may start with your interests and work out to the world, or start with the world's need and work back to yourself. Either way, when you find a need and fill it you are responding to God's call on your life.

This is true even when you're laboring in something short of your dream job. One of Paul's callings was making tents, which paid for his missionary journeys (Acts 18:3). Making tents was not Paul's mission in life, but if I needed a tent I would have bought one from him. Besides its obvious value as a souvenir, I would have trusted the man who wrote, "Whatever you do, work at it with all your heart, as working for the Lord," to have made a sturdy one (Colossians 3:23).

If you're losing excitement for your job, look again at what hunger it's feeding in God's world. What does your job make possible? How does what you do empower others to meet even more needs in God's world? If you can put your finger on that, then you can know that what you have is more than a job. It's a calling from God that provides daily opportunities to bring Him glory. As Gerald Manley Hopkins explained, "To lift up hands in prayer gives God glory, but a man with a dungfork in his hand, a woman with a sloppail, give him glory too. He is so great that all things give him glory if you mean they should."

Did you do that task to please God? Then it brought Him glory, whether it was as small as leading a college or as large as serving your disabled spouse. It all counts now.

Chapter 20

FRUIT

I will not sacrifice to the LORD my God burnt
offerings that cost me nothing.
KING DAVID

Let's review part 2. So far I've said that faith is not a blind leap, where we get ourselves in trouble and wait for God to bail us out. Faith means to commit to what we know, and what we know for sure is what God has revealed in Scripture. We have faith when we trust God enough to try new ventures, but we express just as much faith when we simply claim Scripture's promises and obey its commands.

Scripture's first commandment is to "have no other gods before me" (Exodus 20:3). Luther said we keep this command when we put our faith in Jesus, which then frees us to meet whatever need—large or small—that comes before us. When Luther was a monk he spent all his time and energy trying to save his own soul. But when he received Christ's forgiveness and knew his salvation was secure, he realized he was free to give whatever he had to help others. He didn't need to score points with God by jumping off temples or attempting spiritual feats of strength. It was enough if he served others in the ordinary callings God had assigned to him.

The key to Luther's liberation was twofold: (1) he put his faith in Jesus, and (2) he knew that he had. Only those who *know* they are forgiven by God are free to give themselves away. This brings us to the important question of assurance. I may believe that anyone who repents of his or her sin and trusts Jesus receives God's forgiveness, but I won't rejoice in "the glorious freedom of the children of God" unless I know *I* have done so (Romans 8:21). I may believe that Jesus is the Savior of the world, but how can I tell He has saved *me*?

Assurance is a dangerous topic because the same medicine that restores life to one person might be lethal to the next. There are two kinds of people who lack assurance: those who should and those who shouldn't. Those who *should* lack assurance are the casual Christians who presume that getting baptized or saying the Sinner's Prayer gives them a blank check to live as they please. They know they aren't as godly as they should be, but they assume they're good enough to avoid hell, especially since they once asked Jesus to forgive all their sins. These nonchalant believers need a Christian kick in the pants, which is the goal of this chapter.

However, there are other, more sensitive souls who would be devastated by such tough love. These earnest believers yearn to please God, but they fear their sins are too great to be forgiven. They know that God forgives other, normal folks, but they struggle to believe that He would be willing and able to forgive them. If you are suffocating beneath such a dampening conscience, you should immediately go to the next chapter, which is written especially for you. Everyone else should stuff a magazine in their pants, for what follows might sting.

Are You for Real?

No one likes a hypocrite. Their existence is the number-one reason people give for not going to church. I find hypocrisy as infuriating as the next guy, but whenever someone complains about the hypocrites in church I simply respond, "Of course the church is full of hypocrites. Where else would you find them?"

People only fake what is valuable. Do you know what you'll

never hear? "Larry isn't really a sexual predator. He's just pretend-ing." Or "Sally didn't embezzle the money. She only made it look that way." No one pretends to be a gossip, nag, or pompous wind-bag, because no one wants others to think that's what they are.

Only desirable qualities attract posers, people who want the credit without putting in the work. The guy on the Harley may not really be a tough dude, but his barbed wire tattoo, scruffy beard, and pirate bandana are trying to leave that impression. The young professor wants to be perceived as a serious academic, so she asks you to "terminate the aperture" when she really only wants you to close the window. Dating and social media websites reek with posers—people who pretend to have hair, weigh fifty pounds less, and enjoy fantastic outings with their "amazing" kids.

The next time someone mentions the high number of hypocrites in church, tell them they should take it as a sign that something there is valuable. Fakers flock only to what is good, so consider their preening a reason to take a second look. You must be in the neighborhood of something important. Push past the posers until you find what they are faking.

If it's true that people fake only what is valuable, and if there is nothing more valuable than knowing God, then we must realize that hypocrisy will always be a special temptation for us who love God. The longer we have been Christians, and the better we have been at it, the more we will be tempted to pretend. And this temp-tation will only increase with age. It's the religious leaders, not the new converts, who readily become hypocrites (Matthew 23).

New Christians haven't been saved long enough for others to fully identify them with Jesus. If they quit the church after a few months of faithful attendance, friends and family will shrug it off as a phase. It's more difficult to leave after we've been saved a year. By five years it's clear we've made a commitment. After ten years we'd look foolish to walk away. Some of us have been walking with Jesus for twenty, forty, eighty years. Our whole identity is wrapped up in Jesus; we don't even remember life without Him!

This is a great blessing, but it also provides fertile ground for hypocrisy. If the first thing people say about you is that you're a

Christian—if the opening line of your obituary will say that you went home to be with your Lord—then you have an incentive to keep it going long after your love for Jesus has cooled. Hypocrisy is particularly tempting for pastors and seminary professors. We have a financial incentive to pretend, because if we no longer believe we're going to have to find other jobs. Thank God for your long life of loving Jesus. But never forget that the more godly your reputation, the more you'll be tempted to fake it when it's no longer there.

What's Your Cost?

How can you tell whether or not you're a hypocrite? Jesus said you can tell by your fruit. He said, "Do people pick grapes from thornbushes, or figs from thistles? Likewise every good tree bears good fruit, but a bad tree bears bad fruit" (Matthew 7:16–17).

What makes our fruit good? Jesus said it's not the spectacular ability to prophesy, cast out demons, or perform miracles, for many who do these things will hear from Jesus, "I never knew you. Away from me, you evildoers!" Instead, we bear good fruit whenever we do "the will of my Father who is in heaven" (Matthew 7:21–23).

What is the will of our Father? He wants us to grow in our love for Him, yearning to hear His voice in Scripture (Psalm 119) and replying to Him in prayer (1 Thessalonians 5:17). Toward others, He wants us to bear "the fruit of the Spirit." Rather than give in to the spoiled fruit of "sexual immorality, impurity and debauchery; idolatry and witchcraft; hatred, discord, jealousy, fits of rage, selfish ambition, dissensions, factions and envy; drunkenness, orgies, and the like," His Spirit wants to produce bushels of "love, joy, peace, patience, kindness, goodness, faithfulness, gentleness and self-control" (Galatians 5:19–23).

But how can you tell whether this fruit is genuine? After all, I might do a loving thing not so much for the person I'm helping but to be seen. Recently my daughter's soccer team lost a close match. I knew the game was important to Alayna and that I must be careful how I spoke to her as we walked toward the van. I began by praising her many good plays and how she and the team had improved since their first game, which was true. She perked up, and I congratulated myself on being the compassionate, inspiring father that you read about in the parenting books. She was lucky to have me! Then it hit me. I was more concerned about coming off as a good dad—if only in my own eyes—than about how she felt. This terrified me, for if I can fake love when it comes to the people I care about most, how will I ever know that my love is real?

I get help from Jonathan Edwards, America's greatest theologian. Edwards's most important book is *The Religious Affections*, which he wrote in 1746, two years after the close of the First Great Awakening. This revival had inspired many "lively and powerful" expressions of religious devotion as people swooned, cried out for salvation, shouted praise to God, and recited large chunks of Scripture. Some of these people continued in the faith and became pillars in the church, while others eventually fell away and seemed as lost as ever. Edwards studied both groups and wrote *The Religious Affections* to explain the difference.

Edwards rightly believed that the affections—what he called the "vigorous and sensible exercises of the inclination and will of the soul"—are necessary for a relationship with God. It's not enough to *know* facts about God and the gospel. These truths must *move* you. If you tell the story of Jesus with the emotion of an accountant reading the tax code, then you should take a hard look at the condition of your heart.

But enthusiasm by itself doesn't prove you're a Christian. Edwards used half of *The Religious Affections* to recount the signs that are neither here nor there. Your affections may be "very great." They may come with "fluency and fervor," accompanied by Scripture. They might cause you to faint or erupt in praise. They might fill you with confidence and renewed zeal for your religious duties. But none of this proves your faith is real.

By process of elimination Edwards finally hit upon the key. Near the end of his book he wrote:

> Passing affections easily produce words; and words are
> cheap; and godliness is more easily feigned in words

than in actions. Christian practice is a costly, laborious thing. The self-denial that is required of Christians, and the narrowness of the way that leads to life, does not consist in words, but in practice. Hypocrites may much more easily be brought to talk like saints, than to act like saints.

How can you tell that you're for real? If your faith costs you something. Hypocrites seek maximum press for minimum effort. That's what makes them hypocrites—they're pretending—so they're not going to do anything more than is absolutely required. They will read their Bible, but only to prepare for a lesson. They will pray, but only in front of a group. They will praise their spouse and family, but only in public or on social media, and then they'll belittle and scream at them behind closed doors.

The Christian life takes effort, and that's a good thing; making an effort is the best way to know you're for real. Be glad that blocking out time for prayer and Bible reading is inconvenient. This gives you an opportunity to prove that you really do love God, for we only make time for the people we care about. Rejoice for the opportunity to love your enemy, forgive the friend who wounded you, keep your word when it hurts, swallow the gossip you are dying to share, call in a favor to help someone else, and look away from the barely covered model on your television or computer screen. The burn you feel means you're paying a price, which is something a hypocrite would never do.

What has your faith in Christ cost you? Gladly pay it, and keep the receipt. It's proof that you're for real.

Chapter 21

ASSURANCE

This miry slough is . . . the Slough of Despond:
for still as the sinner is awakened about his lost
condition, there ariseth in his soul many fears,
and doubts, and discouraging apprehensions.
JOHN BUNYAN

Pilgrim's Progress is John Bunyan's classic allegory of Christian's journey to be free from the sin strapped to his back. Christian left the City of Destruction and set off for the Celestial City, but promptly fell into the Slough of Despond. The weight of his burden sank him into the marshy bog, and he would have died if a man named Help hadn't come along and offered a hand (I told you it was an allegory).

Bunyan knew a thing or two about the Slough of Despond. In his autobiography, *Grace Abounding to the Chief of Sinners*, he explained that his tender conscience often acted as a "miry bog." His sinful thoughts would often "sink me into very deep despair, for I concluded that such things could not possibly be found amongst them that loved God."

Bunyan desperately wanted the assurance of salvation, but his incessant second-guessing never let him rest. He knew he would be saved if only he trusted Jesus, but he wondered, *How can I tell I have faith?* Worse, he believed that having faith wouldn't be enough if God had not chosen him for salvation, and so he questioned, *How can I tell I am elected?*

If you are haunted by this last question, take John Calvin's advice to not attempt to "break into the inner recesses of divine wisdom." You can know you are saved if you bear good fruit and, as we will learn in this chapter, fix your eyes on Jesus. Don't try to find yourself in God's decree of election, because as Calvin said, "If we try to penetrate to God's eternal ordination, that deep abyss will swallow us up."

Bunyan's biggest fear was that he had committed the unpardonable sin. Just when he was sure that he "loved Christ dearly," the thought occurred to him that he might want to "exchange him for the things of this life; for any thing." He quickly said no, but the thought returned, and it brought friends. Every day for an entire year Bunyan was besieged with the idea to "Sell Christ for this, or sell Christ for that; sell him, sell him." He refused each time, saying he would not sell Jesus for "thousands, thousands, thousands of worlds." Then one morning, he groggily awakened to the usual temptation and response—"Sell him, sell him, sell him!" "No, no, not for thousands, thousands, thousands, at least twenty times together." But this time, "I felt this thought pass through my heart, 'Let him go if he will!' and I thought also that I felt my heart freely consent thereto."

Oh no! In a moment of weakness Bunyan had agreed to sell Jesus, and now he had lost all hope. He was sure he had crossed the line into damnation, for "My sin was point-blank against my Savior." The "gracious words of the gospel" only worsened his guilt, for it was this compassionate Savior whom he had agreed to sell. No doubt Jesus pitied him, but what could He do for the man who had pushed Him away?

You can read *Grace Abounding* to learn how Bunyan worked through his doubts and eventually gained a measure of assurance, though he never achieved perfect rest. Near the end of the book he

confessed that even "when I have been preaching, I have been vio-
lently assaulted with thoughts of blasphemy, and strongly tempted
to speak them with my mouth before the congregation." Not exactly
the man I want for my pastor! Cover your ears, kids; Pastor Bunyan
is getting crazy eyes!

For our purposes, I want to return to poor Christian drowning
in the Slough of Despond. Have you been there? Have you thought
that your sin is too great to be forgiven? That if the preacher knew
what you had done—and how many times you had done it—he
would not glibly say that Jesus can save you? What is your Help that
will hoist you out of your Slough of Despond? You will survive your
dark night of the soul and gain assurance of your salvation if you
remember to do two things: repent and look.

Repent

I don't know what you did, but if you think your sin is too great
for God to forgive, I've got some bad news for you. You are worse
than you think. On top of all your other sins, you must add one
more: the sin of pride. Do you really think your sin is stronger than
God's grace? Who do you think you are? You may have said no to
God, but your puny "no" will be flicked aside by the roar of God's
YES! He won't even break a sweat.

God was prepared for whatever it was that you did. Not only
was He not surprised by your sin, He was counting on it. Your sin
is precisely why Jesus died. Paul explains: "God made him who
had no sin to be sin for us, so that in him we might become the
righteousness of God" (2 Corinthians 5:21). Jesus became as guilty
as a liar and a cheat, a rapist and a murderer, a child molester and
a gossip, because the guilt of all these sins and more was heaped on
Him. There is no sin you can dream up that He hasn't already suffered, that He hasn't already shredded and scattered across the floor
of His empty tomb.

God didn't sacrifice His Son for small potatoes. He didn't
endure the agony of the cross for people who didn't really need it.

Jesus said, "It is not the healthy who need a doctor, but the sick. I have not come to call the righteous, but sinners to repentance" (Luke 5:31). If you agree that you're a sinner, then you must also agree that you are the target of God's grace, the reason Jesus came to Earth.

Don't be more impressed by yourself than by God. Repent of the sin of thinking your sin can't be forgiven. It's a sin, maybe your biggest one yet. But it's a sin, which means Jesus died for it. Salvation is readily available, if only you'll look.

Look

Where should you look? Last chapter explained that the first place to look is your works: Are you bearing the costly fruit of faith and obedience? This is an important first step, but if we're honest we'll admit that our best fruit is far from perfect. And if we are burdened by a hyperactive conscience, the bruises and blemishes are all we'll see. As Bunyan beat himself up for finally shrugging off Jesus on the millionth temptation, so a sensitive soul will always wonder if its fruit is good enough.

This is why our fruit alone will never put our hearts at ease. The only way to be saved—and to know for sure that you are—is to look to Jesus. Jesus said, "Just as Moses lifted up the snake in the desert, so the Son of Man must be lifted up, that everyone who believes in him may have eternal life" (John 3:14–15). Faith is the mechanism that unites us to Christ. When we believe in Jesus we become one with Him, and His righteousness covers all of the sinful blemishes in our fruit (Philippians 3:9; 1 John 2:24–25).

But what about faith itself? The same sin that prevents us from producing perfect fruit will also prevent us from expressing perfect faith. What if our faith isn't strong enough to lay hold of Jesus and become one with Him? How then can we be saved?

Jesus answers this question by comparing himself to the snake that Moses raised in the desert. When the Israelites were dying of snakebites, God told Moses, "'Make a snake and put it up on a pole; anyone who is bitten can *look* at it and live.' So Moses made a bronze snake and put it up on a pole. Then when anyone was bitten by a snake and *looked* at the bronze snake, he lived" (Numbers 21:8–9).

God uses two Hebrew words for "look" in this passage: *rā'āh* and *nābat*. These words are used interchangeably in the Old Testament, and according to a Hebrew dictionary, *rā'āh* "calls for no special comment, for it is the common word for seeing with the eyes." The dying Israelites didn't have to look at the snake in any special way. Some may have squinted from astigmatism or less than 20/20 vision. Some may have been selfish, pushing past others to get a better look. Some may have doubted, wondering if staring at a bronze snake would really make them well. It didn't matter. The look may have been dim or delayed, but anyone who saw the snake was instantly healed.

Here's what this means for you: the object of your faith is vastly more important than the power of your faith. Your faith may be tiny, fragile, and full of fear. It doesn't matter. Faith is like horseradish—a little goes a long way. Your faith doesn't need to be fancy, it just needs to be well placed. Your faith may be as small as a mustard seed, but if it's in Jesus it's enough to move mountains of guilt and calm the stormy waters of your troubled heart (Matthew 17:20).

As the Israelites with the bronze snake, you don't need to look to Jesus in any special way. You aren't more saved if you pray longer, louder, or with bold confidence. And you aren't less saved if your gaze is shaky and clouded by doubt. Your faith might be "weak" and "imperfect," wrote the author of the Heidelberg Catechism, but it is "nevertheless true and unfeigned." So don't worry about *how* you are looking. Just look, and you are healed. The same Jesus who forgives the sin in your fruit also forgives any flaws in your faith that looks to Him.

Another benefit of looking to Jesus is that it lifts our eyes from ourselves. We won't have time to measure our own shortcomings when we're lost in the ocean of God's love. And any sins that we do notice are easily dispatched. Martin Luther said that whenever

Satan reminded him of his sin, he would answer that he was actually much worse. Luther would say, "Dear devil, I have heard the record. But I have committed still more sins which do not even stand in your record. Put them down, too."

Then Luther would thank Satan for bringing this up, for it gave him an excuse to run to Jesus. He said:

> In fact, when you say that I am a sinner, you provide me with armor and weapons against yourself, so that I may slit your throat with your own sword and trample you underfoot. You yourself are preaching the glory of God to me; for you are reminding me, a miserable and condemned sinner, of the fatherly love of God, who "so loved the world that He gave His only Son, etc." (John 3:16). You are reminding me of the blessing of Christ my Redeemer. On His shoulders, not on mine, lie all my sins. . . . Therefore, when you say that I am a sinner, you do not frighten me; but you bring me immense consolation.

Don't despair over your sin, but use every reminder as a reason to celebrate your salvation. The greater your sin the greater your salvation, so the worse you think you are the more reason you have to thank God.

Are you longing to know you are saved? Look to Jesus. His grace is enough to forgive both the sin in your works and the sin in your faith. Use every pang of guilt as an excuse to run to Him. Do this often enough, and you will become so thankful for His salvation that you will look for ways to express your gratitude. This will inspire you to produce even better fruit, which will bolster your assurance as you see God work through you.

Most important, you can go to bed and sleep soundly, confident that His grace forgives any defects that remain. When Satan reminds you of your sin, thank him for the opportunity to bless Jesus for His boundless love. As Luther said, you'll slit Satan's throat with his own sword, and you'll free yourself to curl up in the cradle of God's grace. Rest in Jesus, and you will learn that assurance of salvation comes the same way as salvation itself—by grace through faith, "not by works, so that no one can boast" (Ephesians 2:8–9).

Chapter 22

HEROES

He who has conquered without danger
has conquered without glory.
Seneca

Many of my college classmates have enjoyed remarkable careers. One is a best-selling author whose stories have been optioned into movies. Another started a ministry to teenage girls and speaks on purity throughout the world. Others have become mayors, pastors, and missionaries to Mongolia, Germany, and Australia. I know about these friends because they are often featured in my alumni magazine, which is properly proud of their success.

I have other classmates who I hear about less, in part because they duck whenever the college shines its searchlight in their direction. Some are unemployed, sick, or divorced. They scrape through life, determined to give their kids a shot at the dream they once had. For various reasons—some self-inflicted and others imposed upon them—life hasn't turned out as they had hoped.

Which group sounds more like champions of faith? Which has the best shot of making it into God's Hall of Fame? If the list in Hebrews chapter 11 is any indication, it's hard to say. Great faith isn't always met with unmistakable success.

Keeping Faith

Hebrews is one of the more puzzling books of the Bible. We don't even know who wrote it, but we do know it was written to encourage Christians to persevere in their faith. Perseverance can be a controversial doctrine. Some Christians argue for the "total security" of the believer, citing Jesus' promise that His sheep "shall never perish" (John 10:28–30) and Paul's assurance that "he who began a good work in you will carry it on to completion until the day of Christ Jesus" (Philippians 1:6). Others point to Hebrews' warnings against falling away from the faith, saying that God wouldn't warn us against something that wasn't possible (6:4–6; 10:26–31).

Personally, I'm attracted to the comfort that comes from knowing my salvation is secure. As Luther said, if salvation was in my hands I am sure I would drop it. I prefer the phrase "perseverance of the saints" to "total security," for the former implies there is work for me to do. I can't kick back, sin as I please, and still take comfort that I am "totally secure." My perseverance rests in God's hands, yet it requires effort on my part. Paul grounded my effort in God's power when he encouraged believers "to work out your salvation with fear and trembling, for it is God who works in you to will and to act according to his good purpose" (Philippians 2:12–13).

One helpful answer on the question of perseverance comes from my New Testament colleague David Turner. When asked if he thought it was possible to lose our salvation, he replied, "Let's not find out." Why do we even care to know where God draws the line? Let's not make our final judgment a toss-up, an excruciatingly close call for God to make, but let's live such godly, grace-fueled lives that the question becomes moot.

Hebrews addresses perseverance because it was written to people who noticed the gap between what they saw and what they believed. Hebrews emphasizes what we believe about Jesus, that He has fulfilled the longings of God's people by defeating the powers of evil, securing our salvation, and is now interceding for us at the Father's right hand (2:14; 7:25–28; 9:23–28). But that's the prob-

lem. Because Jesus is in heaven, we don't see Him. We see mostly
trouble, an unruly world treating God's people with contempt (2:8;
10:32–34).

We will only persevere if we "encourage one another daily" to "fix
[our] thoughts on Jesus," drawing "near to God with a sincere heart
in full assurance of faith" (3:1, 13; 10:22). Only faith can bridge the
gap between what we see and what we believe. And so Hebrews, in
its quest to encourage us to "run with perseverance the race marked
out for us" (12:1) includes history's greatest chapter on faith.

Power of Faith

The eleventh chapter of Hebrews begins with this famous
description: "Now faith is being sure of what we hope for and
certain of what we do not see." This is not a definition of faith—
remember that faith means to commit to what we know—rather
it's a description of what faith does. When we trust what God has
revealed, we bring the future into the present ("sure of what we
hope for") and make the invisible world visible ("certain of what we
do not see").

Faith is your ticket to the show. The performance hasn't happened yet, so there is nothing to see, but your glossy ticket is proof
that you will be there when it does. The greatest show on Earth is
the return of the King. Angels will trumpet His arrival as glorified
saints burst out of their graves with shouts of joy and laughter. They
will converge on Jesus, who with the armies of heaven will wrestle
evil to the ground once and for all (Revelation 19:11–21).

Your ticket to this show—your guarantee that you will rise to
greet your King—is your faith in His Word. Hebrews declares this
Word "is living and active. Sharper than any double-edged sword,
it penetrates even to dividing soul and spirit, joints and marrow;
it judges the thoughts and attitudes of the heart" (4:12). But this
Word will not help us if we do "not combine it with faith" (4:2).
We must "not refuse him who speaks," or we will "not escape"
when the "consuming fire" of Jesus returns to "shake . . . the earth"
(12:25–29).

By now you won't be surprised that Martin Luther had something to say about this aspect of faith. Luther said we must choose whether we're going to be theologians of glory or theologians of the cross. The former use reason to look for God in the obvious places: the power of a storm or the stop-what-you're-doing-and-look beauty of a sunset or rainbow. But where do we most clearly see God? Not in these likely suspects but in the excruciating shame of the cross. God most powerfully reveals himself as the naked, tortured man gasping for air before a jeering mob. When it looks like God isn't even in the neighborhood, that is exactly where we find Him.

This revelation of the cross inspired Luther to emphasize the shocking, improbable nature of God's Word. He warned that we must not trust our eyes, for looks can be deceiving. Rather we must use the Word of God that we hear to interpret what we see. Your eyes tell you that you are a sinner, but God's Word says that your Father looks at you through the righteousness of His Son and declares that you're a saint (2 Corinthians 1:1; 5:21). Your eyes tell you that the loved one you buried is never coming back, but the Word of God promises that you are standing on resurrection ground. At any moment Jesus will return, raise your beloved, and live forever with both of you in this new, redeemed world. Faith relies on its ears rather than its eyes, which is why Protestant churches follow Luther's lead and make the sermon the center of their worship service. "Faith comes from hearing the message," said Paul, "and the message is heard through the word of Christ" (Romans 10:17).

Luther added that the Word of God not only promises incredible events but it powerfully delivers on these promises. The Word of God makes things happen. God's Word created the universe, delivers sinners from death to life, raises the dead, and on the last day will destroy God's enemies and restore this shattered world (Hebrews 11:3; 1 Peter 1:23; John 11:43; Revelation 19:15; 21:5).

The total triumph of God's Word takes the pressure from our shoulders. We no longer bear the impossible burden of trying to achieve lasting security and significance on our own, which is as futile as trying to build a house of salt on water. Rather we realize that the only force that has staying power is the Word of God, and so we gladly commit our life and death to Him, trusting Him to raise us on the day He returns.

Stories of Faith

This complete dependence on the Word of God is the one constant in Hebrews 11. Abel, Enoch, Noah, and all the rest demonstrated their faith by either claiming God's promise or obeying His command. Consider Abraham, our father of faith. He obeyed God's command to leave his homeland and settle in a foreign country, and he claimed God's promise that he and Sarah, though too old to bear children, would have "descendants as numerous as the stars in the sky and as countless as the sand on the seashore" (Hebrews 11:8–12). He combined both God's promise and command when he bound Isaac on the altar. He raised his knife in the hope "that God could raise the dead" (Hebrews 11:17–19).

Many of these heroes enjoyed fantastic success. They "conquered kingdoms . . . shut the mouths of lions, quenched the fury of the flames, and escaped the edge of the sword." They "became powerful in battle and routed foreign armies. Women received back their dead, raised to life again." However, "Others were tortured. . . . Some faced jeers and flogging, while still others were chained and put in prison. They were stoned; they were sawed in two; they were put to death by the sword. They went about in sheepskins and goatskins, destitute, persecuted and mistreated—the world was not worthy of them. They wandered in deserts and mountains, and in caves and holes in the ground" (Hebrews 11:33–38).

Why are both groups—those who miraculously triumphed and those who apparently failed—included as heroes of faith? Because faith is not measured by what we do but by our trust in what God has done and will yet do. We all share the same promise, that Jesus "has appeared once for all at the end of the ages to do away with sin" and that "he will appear a second time, not to bear sin, but to bring salvation to those who are waiting for him" (Hebrews 9:26–28). None of the heroes in Hebrews lived long enough to see this promise, but they all died believing that God's Word would come true (Hebrews 11:13, 39).

We are in the very same boat. Hebrews does not tell us to prove ourselves by attempting spectacular leaps of faith, which in many sermons and books amounts to taking large financial risks. In two chapters of application, Hebrews mentions money only once. The author doesn't encourage us to plant seed money in hopes that God will repay us sevenfold, but merely to "Keep your lives free from the love of money and be content with what you have" (13:5).

The expectations in Hebrews chapters 12 and 13 are rather ordinary: "live in peace with all men" and "be holy" (12:14), avoid bitterness and sexual immorality (12:15–16), "keep on loving each other" (13:1), "entertain strangers" (13:2), "do not forget to do good and to share with others" (13:16), and "obey your leaders and submit to their authority" (13:17). Basic stuff. Every Christian can do these, whether they are megachurch pastors or unemployed homeless people.

And that's the point. I don't know whether God has abundantly blessed your life or whether you are just scraping by. I do know that you can be a man or woman of faith if only you will lift your eyes from your own circumstances, claim God's promise, and obey His commands. You can be one of God's heroes, whether your home is a castle or a hole in the ground.

Chapter 23

BELIEVE

Everything is possible for him who believes.
JESUS

If there is a poster boy for the leap of faith, it would have to be Felix Baumgartner. On October 14, 2012, this Austrian daredevil stepped out of a space capsule twenty-four miles up and plummeted toward Earth. "It's almost overwhelming," Baumgartner told the BBC after one of his test flights. "When you're standing there in a pressure suit, the only thing that you hear is yourself breathing, and you can see the curvature of the Earth; you can see the sky's totally black. It's kind of an awkward view because you've never seen a black sky. And at that moment, you realise you've accomplished something really big."

Baumgartner prepared five years for his leap into space, but there were many questions that could not be answered until he jumped. Would breaking the sound barrier knock him unconscious? Would he turn into a fireball? Baumgartner did tumble head over feet for several seconds—at 834 mph—but fortunately he managed to right himself and release his parachute.

Baumgartner's leap was literally out of this world, which made his answer in a post-jump interview particularly intriguing. One fan asked if he would have jumped if there were only a 50 percent chance that he would survive. Baumgartner replied, "Never. If I do something, it's always 90 percent obvious and 10 percent unknown. Fifty-fifty means you get the same chance to die as to survive. I'd never work that way. That would be stupid."

Did you catch that? Even daredevils, if they want to stick around, don't wish upon a star and go for it. Baumgartner prepared for years with a team of experts before he was ready for his historic jump. I'm not sure his odds were as high as he thought, but I respect that his risk was calculated. Baumgartner has jumped more often from higher platforms than any of us ever will, yet even he admits that faith is a commitment to what we know. The more spectacular the leap, the more important it is to ground that leap in knowledge.

Believe in Yourself?

This wisdom is largely lost on our culture, which promotes a sort of existential narcissism. Most popular treatments of faith say it doesn't matter what you believe or if you have good reason for believing it. Just believe something—whatever you want—and you'll find that the sheer act of believing will propel you to greatness. Consider Josh Groban's hit song "Believe." This mellow ballad sets the mood for the Christmas movie *The Polar Express*, which teaches the ability of faith to alter reality. Near the end of the movie there is a silver bell. Does it ring? Well, that depends. If you are a child who believes in Christmas, then the bell rings, but if you're a rational, stuffy adult, then it doesn't. So our minds have the power to change reality? We can make bells ring just by thinking they do?

Groban's ballad encourages us to reclaim our magical powers on Christmas day. It sounds better when he sings it, but here is the chorus:

> Believe in what your heart is saying
> Hear the melody that's playing
> There's no time to waste
> There's so much to celebrate
> Believe in what you feel inside

And give your dreams the wings to fly
You have everything you need
If you just believe

The message is clear: You can do anything as long as you believe. The city of Orlando was built on this idea. Recently I took my family to Sea World, which is one of the favorite places from my childhood. Actually it's still one of my favorite places. The theme of the Shamu Show was "Believe," and its theme song encouraged us to "break free" in our "magic moment" and "see the world through the eyes of a child." We must:

Believe, what we see can be somehow
Believe, that this moment is happening now
Believe

One of the trainers gave a long speech about the need to believe in yourself, and then he interviewed a child, who said her dream was to grow up and become a whale trainer. Everyone clapped, not because they thought this would actually happen but simply because the child had enough sense to believe what she was told. My son, Avery, apparently the cynical one in our family, observed that the Orca tail necklace that the trainer dramatically hung around the child's neck as a reminder to believe in herself was also being hawked to put-upon parents for five dollars immediately after the show. He also noted that due to a recent tragedy, the trainers are no longer permitted to get in the water with Shamu. So maybe they still believed in themselves, but apparently their employer didn't.

We went across town to the Magic Kingdom, where frequent parades reminded us to believe in ourselves and celebrate our dreams, "whatever they are." My son said his dream was to take over the world. Should that be celebrated? My dream was for free refills on soda, but that was dashed at the cashier's stand less than ten minutes after the last float danced by.

As we left the park the loudspeakers played a happy song with the chorus, "In everything you do, celebrate you!" I understand why

Disney does this. It's good business to sell smiles and self-esteem, as no one would hang out in a place that berated them for their shortcomings. Disney is an amusement park, and the quickest way to amuse someone is to play catchy songs that say they're great. I get that, but it's still worth pointing out that this endlessly narcissistic message will destroy anyone who attempts to live it. The poor fellow who follows the advice, "In everything you do, celebrate you!" won't be married long. And he won't have many friends.

Worse, as I explained in chapter 13, we die with whatever we have lived for. If we put our faith in ourselves, then we will receive whatever help we can offer at the moment of death. But we will be *dying*, so we will be no help at all. Why would anyone commit to a plan that is guaranteed to fail, especially when the consequence of failure is hell?

Raise the Risk?

We Christians know enough to put our faith in God, though sometimes I wonder if our faith knows enough. Some Christians can be so impressed by the uncertainty of their knowledge that they concede too much. One philosopher rightly observes that while he cannot prove the Christian faith to others he is still rationally permitted to believe it. But then he writes: "I'll settle for rational permissibility. That way I can know that my faith is not blind. I may be taking a leap in the dim, but it is not a leap in the dark. Leaping is still risky business, but in faith, I hope that God will make my landing soft." I appreciate his humility, but don't you want to say more about what you believe? Is it enough to say that your faith is rational? Don't you also want to say that you know you're right?

This is what I attempted to show in part 1. Our faith is not a leap into the dark, or even into the dim, but into the bright light of God's Word. Scripture assures us that we're not only allowed to believe in the Christian God but also that we are *right* to believe in Him. We know that God exists; He has stamped His image upon us and planted the knowledge of himself within us. Romans chapter 1 says that God has done this for everyone, so no one can say they do not know that an almighty, good God exists.

The existence of this righteous God should prompt every sinner to search for grace, which can be found in only one place. We may say we don't know that Jesus is God, but we can't deny that He is precisely what we know we need. I know that Jesus is God's Son because I learn about Him in Scripture, which proves itself to be the Word of God when I read it. I don't pretend this argument will persuade those who have not received the witness of the Spirit. But I can't deny that the Spirit opens my ears to hear God's voice when I read His Word, and He uses what I learn there to assure me that I am God's child (Romans 8:16).

As I discussed in chapter 8, if this has not yet happened to you, then you must throw yourself on the mercy of God. Open your Bible to the gospel of John and implore God to speak to you. God "rewards those who earnestly seek him," so if you are willing to do whatever He tells you, He will keep His promise and meet you there (Hebrews 11:6).

If some Christians emphasize the uncertainty of believing in God, others stress the need for uncertainty in following God. They suggest we are too comfortable in our secure, middle-class lifestyles and that we best live for Jesus when we attempt large, risky acts in His name. They say, "We were created for more, far more" than merely "avoiding badness and providing for the family." We must not waste our lives on a normal, mundane existence, for "risk is right."

I need to hear this challenge to complacency, for it's too easy to adjust my spiritual passion to the temperature of those around me. As long as I'm somewhere in the middle of the pack, no more materialistic than the average Christian, I assume I'm doing okay. And yet, while I must continually monitor my status quo, I question whether the amount of my risk is the way to measure the size of my faith. This is what I attempted to show in part 2.

Our problem is sin, not comfort. Comfort can easily become an idol that we pursue above God, but a comfortable, middle-class existence is not necessarily an indication of sin. It may simply mean we're prudent. Paul never commanded Christians to take radical risks for God. He was content if they avoided immorality and quietly worked hard at their jobs (1 Thessalonians 4:1–12). You might think this lowers the bar of the Christian life, but imagine the church's witness if we actually met it!

Rather than focus on how much we're risking for God, we should concentrate on God's promises and commands. Are you trusting all of His promises and obeying all of His commands? Are you doing everything God has called you to do? If you are, then you are a person of faith. Don't beat yourself up if you have some money left over or you enjoy your home. A good life may be a sign of God's favor, not of your sin.

The Gift of Faith

The point of this book is that faith means to commit to what we know, not to what we don't. So the foundational question, the question that will lift your faith off the ground, is, What do you know? If you're not sure what you know, ask yourself what you believe. Are these beliefs true, and do you have good reason for holding them? Then you are entitled to claim that you know them. And once you realize that you know them, you are obligated to commit appropriately to them.

I understand that the journey of faith is different for each of us, and the biblical passages and arguments that strengthen my faith may leave you unconvinced. Perhaps you feel encouraged by what you read in this book, but the same doubts that squeezed your heart at the start are still gripping your chest at the end. Perhaps you still aren't persuaded that you know enough to believe.

If this describes you, I want you to leave you with two thoughts. First, the end of this book is not the end of your quest. You may not have resolved all of your questions here, but I pray you are further ahead than when you began. Don't give up, but pursue your answers in hope. Second, while faith in God is the most natural act in the world, none of us will believe without supernatural help.

Faith is natural because we already know a lot about God from the world He has made. Yet because we sinfully suppress and distort this truth, we all need God to overcome our blindness and draw us to himself.

Jesus pondered why some people believe and others don't and concluded that the difference was God. He said, "no one can come to me unless the Father has enabled him" (John 6:65), and "no one knows the Father except the Son and those to whom the Son chooses to reveal him" (Matthew 11:27). You might think this supplies an excuse to shrug and sit on our hands, waiting for God to make everything clear. But in the very next verse Jesus issues an invitation that doubles as a command: "Come to me, all you who are weary and burdened, and I will give you rest. Take my yoke upon you and learn from me, for I am gentle and humble in heart, and you will find rest for your souls" (vv. 28–29).

Are you weary of wrestling with doubts? Come.

Are you burdened by the crushing fear that you could be wrong? Just come.

Don't wait until you have everything figured out, because that day will never come. Jesus invites "you who are weary and burdened" to come. Come with your struggles, doubts, and fears. Come with your outrage, shock, and tears. Jesus' shoulders have borne the sin of the world; they're broad enough for whatever you're carrying.

When Martin Luther struggled with doubt he reminded himself that belief in God was a command, and the very first one. This command liberated him to believe out of obedience until he could believe out of firm and certain knowledge. And that knowledge was sure to come, for Jesus said, "If anyone chooses to do God's will, he will find out whether my teaching comes from God" (John 7:17). Obey the truth, and you will eventually come to know even more truth. You will know more than enough to believe, more than enough to put your doubt away.

DISCUSSION
QUESTIONS

If you are reading this page, you are either using this book in a small group setting or you're an attentive reader who desires to go deeper. Either way, I'd like to assist you by explaining the outline of this book.

This book has two parts. Part 1 addresses the doubts we have about the *objects* of our faith: God, Jesus, and Scripture. Part 2 examines the doubts we have about the *quality* of our faith: Have we really believed in Jesus? How do we know we're following Him? How can we tell we're saved?

After an introductory first chapter, both parts follow the same structure, as presented here.

	Part 1	*Part 2*
Why faith is hard:	Chapters 2–3	Chapter 14
How ignorance makes faith impossible:	Chapter 4	Chapter 15
How knowledge makes faith possible:	Chapter 5	Chapter 16
What faith can know:	Chapters 6–8	Chapters 17–19
How doubters can gain assurance:	Chapters 9–12	Chapters 20–22
Invitation to believe:	Chapter 13	Chapter 23

With this big picture in mind, here are questions to help you better understand and apply the content of this book.

Chapter 1: Doubt Away

1. What doubt troubles you the most? Why is this doubt so upsetting? Where can you turn for help?
2. Do you doubt too much or too little? If you had to pick one, would you say you are more skeptical or more naïve? How would your friends describe you?
3. Recall a time when you felt overwhelmed by doubt. How did you work through it? Did you learn anything—either what to do or what not to do—that you can apply to your struggles now?

Chapter 2: Skepticism

1. Are you satisfied with your prayer life? What might the amount and quality of our prayers indicate about our faith?
2. Is it important for you to prove what you believe? What do you find easy to believe without proof? How might this apply to your belief in God?
3. Has modern science produced more or less reason to believe in God? Give examples of each.

Chapter 3: Pluralism

1. Why is it important to put your faith in what you know?
2. How would you respond to a friend who says you can't know anything about God?
3. Which is worse, to say there is no God or there is a God but we can't know Him?

Chapter 4: Leap

1. How would you describe the relationship between faith and doubt? Is doubt necessary for faith, is doubt the opposite of faith, or is there a third option?
2. Do you know anyone who took a blind "leap of faith"? How did it turn out?
3. Would you find it easier to love and obey God if you heard His voice thundering from heaven? Why or why not?

Chapter 5: Knowledge

1. Write down one thing you know for sure. What makes you sure this fact is true? Is there a lesson here that you can apply to your faith in God?

2. Do you struggle more with the intellectual or volitional side of faith? In other words, is it more difficult for you to know what to believe or to commit to what you know?

3. Do doubts about God say more about Him or the person who has them?

Chapter 6: God

1. Do you have enough certainty to believe in God? If not, what would it take to convince you that He exists? Do you think your request would sound reasonable to God?

2. Do you agree that everyone innately knows that God exists? Why or why not?

3. Did you say or do anything today that would be meaningless if God did not exist? What does that tell you about what you believe about God?

Chapter 7: Jesus

1. What might you say to a friend who believes in God but not Jesus?

2. If you were on trial for believing in Jesus, would there be enough evidence to convict you?

3. Many people believe that a variety of religions can save you as long as you are sincere. What does this popular viewpoint imply about the necessity of Jesus?

Chapter 8: Bible

1. How can we know that God has spoken in Scripture?

2. Scripture is God's message to you. What you do with that Word is your message to Him. What message are you sending?

3. What would you say to a person who declares that God has opened his or her heart to see a book other than the Bible as

God's revelation? You both appeal to a witness of the Spirit and you both assume you are right. What might you say to break the stalemate?

Chapter 9: Belief

1. If it's true that our choices and actions influence our beliefs, what have your choices, for better or for worse, set you up to believe?
2. How might viewing pornography, having an affair, or nursing a grudge influence your beliefs about God?
3. Think of a doubt you currently have. How can you tell if it's an honest doubt or disobedience masquerading as doubt?

Chapter 10: Quest

1. If you're feeling overwhelmed by doubt, try flipping the script. Pretend you don't believe in God, Jesus, or the Bible. What new doubts must you struggle with then?
2. What steps can you take to maintain a thankful, hopeful attitude despite your doubt?
3. Can you think of a belief that you hold more strongly because you worked through your doubts about it?

Chapter 11: Unbelief

1. Given the fact of our sin, do you think it is possible to have an entirely honest doubt?
2. Do you sin more from doubt or disobedience—because you aren't sure what God wants or because you don't care?
3. Our faith tends to acclimate to the temperature of our friends. Do you need to consider who you spend time with?

Chapter 12: Disciplines

1. Does your use of technology support or hinder your belief in God? Do you find it easier to believe the more time you spend online?

2. What spiritual disciplines have strengthened your faith (e.g., church participation, Bible reading, prayer, fasting, giving, serving)? Are you doing them now? Which do you need to recommit to?

3. Although our faith must be our own, why is it difficult to believe on our own?

Chapter 13: Faith

1. What would your family and friends say you are living for? Would you agree?

2. Which is a larger risk, believing in Jesus or believing in something else?

3. What good thing are you most tempted to turn into an idol? How will you prevent this gift from God from usurping His place?

Chapter 14: Trust

1. How can you tell if you are relying on Jesus?

2. What is your backup plan? Are you more tempted to rely on people or on things, such as money or a job? How can you destroy the plan without damaging the people or job that have supplied your false sense of security?

3. Why is the discipline of giving a great way to eliminate backup plans?

Chapter 15: Jump

1. What does it mean to live by faith? How important is it that faith attempts something spectacular?

2. Which requires faith: to sell your possessions and become a missionary in a foreign country or to support your family by dependably showing up for your regular job?

3. How can you tell if your "leap of faith" is *from* security or *for* security? Why is it a sin to test God's love for you?

Chapter 16: Faithfulness

1. How is the voice of God similar to and different from the voice of your conscience? How can you tell if you are hearing from God or being convicted by your conscience?
2. Do you agree that God does not hold us responsible for ignoring what we don't know is from Him? Why or why not? Do we sin when we don't obey what we believe is from Him?
3. Some claims to God's voice are dubious. What would you say to a wealthy man who claimed God was leading him to walk away from his mortgage?

Chapter 17: Promise

1. Why might it have been an act of faith for Mark not to loan the money to the mission? If both giving and not giving are equally acceptable, how can you determine what and when to give?
2. Are you glad that God has left the amount and recipients of your giving up to you? Or do you wish He would tell you exactly how much to give to whom? What does your record of giving say about your faith? Does the Old Testament practice of tithing influence your decision?
3. How do you reconcile God's command to "Test me in this" (Malachi 3:10) with Jesus' statement that it is a sin to "put the Lord your God to the test" (Matthew 4:7)? Hint: Does it matter if the test is a response to a promise or command from God?

Chapter 18: Command

1. What does Scripture teach you to value most? List your top three values. Do your values inform your decisions?
2. Do you think it's important to receive God's direction outside the pages of Scripture? Why or why not?
3. Martin Luther said to obey the first commandment, and "then do whatever comes before you." Do you find this idea unnerving or freeing? Why?

Chapter 19: Call

1. Why is the ordeal of Robertson and Muriel such a compelling love story? What does their story teach us about the value of our trials?
2. List your top five callings. Which ones are you doing well, and which do you need to commit to doing better?
3. Have you answered all of God's callings on your life? How can you tell if He is calling you into a new vocation?

Chapter 20: Fruit

1. What sacrifices have you made to follow Jesus? Have you seen enough fruit in your life to know your faith is real?
2. What sacrifice are you reluctant to make? How might the cost actually provide an incentive to do it?
3. What would you *start* doing if you knew others would find out? What would you *stop* doing if you knew others would find out?

Chapter 21: Assurance

1. Do you find it difficult to receive God's forgiveness? How can you turn the reminder of your sin into a celebration of Jesus?
2. Why is looking to Jesus even more important than looking to our fruit to gain assurance?
3. Why do you think Jesus compared himself to a snake? What does that analogy tell you about your salvation and how it was provided? (See 2 Corinthians 5:21.)

Chapter 22: Heroes

1. Take a moment to think about your life. What promise from God do you most need to claim and what command do you most need to obey?
2. Do you find it easier to live by faith—trusting God's promises and following His commands—when life is difficult or when things are going well? Why do you think that is?

3. What does Paul mean when he says, "you have been given fullness in Christ"? (Colossians 2:10). How might this fact enable you to remain content regardless of the circumstances of life?

Chapter 23: Believe

1. Can you think of an example from your culture that encourages people to simply believe in themselves? Why is this an example of misplaced faith?
2. *This I Believe*, a nonprofit organization, invites entries for its weekly radio program. Write a 350–500 word essay that explains your most cherished beliefs and consider entering it at thisibelieve.org.
3. How has this book challenged your prior understanding of doubt and faith? What outstanding questions do you still have? Please write or e-mail me in care of the publisher (see Note to the Reader at the back of the book).

SOURCES

Chapter 1: Doubt Away

Frederick Buechner, *Wishful Thinking: A Theological ABC* (San Francisco: Harper & Row, 1973), 20.

Chapter 2: Skepticism

Charles Taylor, *A Secular Age* (Cambridge, MA: Harvard University Press, 2007).

Chapter 3: Pluralism

Lisa Miller, "We Are All Hindus Now," *Newsweek* (August 14, 2009). Accessed online at http://www.thedailybeast.com/newsweek/2009/08/14/we-are-all-hindus-now.html.

The Pew Forum survey, "Many Americans Say Other Faiths Can Lead to Eternal Life" (December 18, 2008), is available online at http://www.pewforum.org/Many-Americans-Say-Other-Faiths-Can-Lead-to-Eternal-Life.aspx.

LaTonya Taylor, "The Church of O," *Christianity Today,* April 1, 2002, accessed online at http://www.christianitytoday.com/ct/2002/april1/1.38.html. Oprah's description of God, which closed the final episode of her popular talk show, can be found at http://religion.blogs.cnn.com/2011/05/25/oprah-says-god-behind-success-of-show/.

Elizabeth Gilbert, *Eat, Pray, Love* (New York: Viking Penguin, 2006), 13–16.

Chapter 4: Leap

Gilbert, *Eat, Pray, Love*, 13–16, 141, 175.

John Ortberg, *Faith and Doubt* (Grand Rapids: Zondervan, 2008), 137–39.

Chapter 5: Knowledge

Anselm, "Proslogion," in *Anselm of Canterbury: The Major Works,* ed. Brian Davies and G. R. Evans (New York: Oxford University Press, 1998), 87.

For the Bernie Madoff story, see Robert Chew, "How I Got Screwed by Bernie Madoff," *Time* (Monday, December 15, 2008), available at http://www.time.com/time/business/article/0,8599,1866398,00.html; and Kim Christensen, "Their Safe Bet Had Bet It All on Madoff," *The Los Angeles Times* (December 21, 2008), available at http://articles.latimes.com/2008/dec/21/business/fi-madoff-chais21.

Ronald M. Green, *Kierkegaard and Kant: The Hidden Debt* (Albany: State University of New York Press, 1992), 132–46 and C. Stephen Evans, *Faith Beyond Reason: A Kierkegaardian Account* (Grand Rapids: Eerdmans, 1998), 65–113.

John Calvin, *The Institutes of the Christian Religion* 3.2.7–8, ed. John T. McNeill, trans. Ford Lewis Battles (Philadelphia: Westminster, 1960), 551–52.

Heidelberg Catechism, Q. and A. 21, in *Ecumenical Creeds and Reformed Confessions* (Grand Rapids: CRC Publications, 1988), 19. I replace "deep-rooted assurance" with "hearty trust," which is my translation of the German phrase *ein herzliches Vertrauen.*

Chapter 6: God

You can read the Wilson-Hitchens debate at http://www.christianitytoday.com/ct/2007/mayweb-only/119-12.0.html.

For the argument for God from rationality, see Alvin Plantinga, "Justification and Theism," *Faith and Philosophy* 4 (1987): 403–26; *Warrant and Proper Function* (New York: Oxford University Press, 1993), 216–37; *Warranted Christian Belief* (New York: Oxford University Press, 2000), 227–40; "Naturalism Defeated," available at http://www.calvin.edu/academic/philosophy/virtual_library/articles/plantinga_alvin/naturalism_defeated.pdf; and "Against Naturalism," in Alvin Plantinga and Michael Tooley, *Knowledge of God* (Hoboken, NJ: Wiley-Blackwell, 2008) 1–69.

C. S. Lewis, *Miracles: A Preliminary Study* (New York: MacMillan, 1978), 12–24; C. S. Lewis, *Christian Reflections,* ed. Walter Hooper (1967; repr., Grand Rapids: Eerdmans, 1989), 63–71; Victor Reppert, *C. S. Lewis' Dangerous Idea* (Downers Grove, IL: InterVarsity Press, 2003).

Information on our genetic code comes from a lecture by Mark Hughes, "The Human Embryo: Diagnosing Disease, Cloning, Stem Cell Research: We Can, but Should We?" at The January Series of Calvin College, Grand Rapids, MI, January 19, 2001.

John Calvin, *Institutes* 1.3.1, pp. 43–44.

Caleb Miller, "Faith and Reason," in *Reason for the Hope Within,* ed. Michael J. Murray (Grand Rapids: Eerdmans, 1999), 149.

Douglas Wilson, "Christopher Hitchens Has Died, Douglas Wilson Reflects," *Christianity Today,* December 16, 2011, available at http://www.christianitytoday.com/ct/2011/decemberweb-only/christopher-hitchens-obituary.html.

Chapter 7: Jesus

Charles W. Colson, *Born Again* (Old Tappan, NJ: Chosen Books, 1976), 49–71, 109–30.

Jonathan Aitken, "Transformed," *Christianity Today,* June 2012, 53–55.

Graham Cole, *He Who Gives Life* (Wheaton: Crossway, 2007), 166–67.

Chapter 8: Bible

Carl Sagan, *Contact* (1985; repr., New York: Pocket Books, 1997), 36, 158–73, 371–82.

Alvin Plantinga, *Where the Conflict Really Lies* (New York: Oxford University Press, 2011), 59.

John Calvin, *Institutes* 1.7.2 and 1.7.4, pp. 76, 79.

Chapter 9: Belief

Martin Luther, "Preface to the Epistle of St. Paul to the Romans," *Luther's Works,* ed. E. Theodore Bachmann and Helmut T. Lehmann (Philadelphia: Muhlenberg Press, 1960), 35:370.

Chapter 10: Quest

Martin Luther, WA 40.ii.15.15, in *The Righteousness of God: Luther Studies,* trans. E. Gordon Rupp (London: Hodder and Stoughton, 1953), 104, and quoted in David C. Steinmetz, *Luther in Context,* 2nd ed. (Grand Rapids: Baker, 2002), 2.

Heiko A. Oberman, *Luther: Man Between God and the Devil*, trans. Eileen Walliser-Schwarzbart (New York: Image Books, 1982; English edition, 1992), 147.

Roland Bainton, *Here I Stand: A Life of Martin Luther* (New York: Abingdon-Cokesbury Press, 1950), 78, 185.

Martin Brecht, *Martin Luther: His Road to Reformation, 1483–1521*, trans. James L. Schaaf (Philadelphia: Fortress Press, 1981; English edition, 1985), 460.

Chapter 11: Unbelief

Karl Barth, *Church Dogmatics* IV.1, trans. G. W. Bromiley (1956; repr., Edinburgh: T. & T. Clark, 1997), 291–94.

James S. Spiegel, *The Making of an Atheist: How Immorality Leads to Unbelief* (Chicago: Moody Press, 2010), 73, 85.

Joseph Levine, "From Yeshiva Bochur to Secular Humanist," in *Philosophers Without Gods: Meditations on Atheism and the Secular Life*, ed. Louise M. Antony (New York: Oxford University Press, 2007), 17–30.

Cornelius Plantinga Jr., *Not the Way It's Supposed to Be: A Breviary of Sin* (Grand Rapids: Eerdmans, 1995), 105–7.

Chapter 12: Disciplines

Heidelberg Catechism, Q. 65, in *Ecumenical Creeds and Reformed Confessions* (Grand Rapids: CRC Publications, 1988), 41.

Paul Althaus, *The Theology of Martin Luther*, trans. Robert C. Schultz (Philadelphia: Fortress Press, 1966), 316–18.

Dietrich Bonhoeffer, *Dietrich Bonhoeffer Works*, vol. 1, *Sanctorum Communio: A Theological Study of the Sociology of the Church*, ed. Joachim von Soosten; English edition, ed. Clifford J. Green, trans. Reihard Krauss and Nancy Lukens (Minneapolis: Fortress Press, 1998), 229–30.

John Calvin, *Institutes* 4.14.1, p. 1277.

Lewis, *Christian Reflections*, 42.

Chapter 13: Faith

Walter Isaacson, *Steve Jobs* (New York: Simon & Schuster, 2011), xx, 453–56, 570–71.

Chapter 14: Trust

Tim Keller, *Counterfeit Gods* (New York: Dutton, 2009), xvii–xviii.

Chapter 15: Jump

Henry T. Blackaby and Claude V. King, *Experiencing God* (Nashville: Broadman & Holman, 1994), 133–34, 138.

William Carey, "Brief Narrative of the Baptist Mission in India," 5th ed. (London: Button & Son, 1819), 3. Accessed online at http://www .wmcarey.edu/carey/baptmiss1819/3.jpg. For a literary history of Carey's famous quote, see http://www.wmcarey.edu/carey/expect/.

Bruce Wilkinson, *The Prayer of Jabez* (Sisters, OR: Multnomah, 2000), 15–16, 33–34, 47.

Chapter 16: Faithfulness

Blackaby, *Experiencing God*, 87–89, 92, 167.

John Bowlby, *A Secure Base* (New York: Basic Books, 1988), 11.

Chapter 18: Command

Martin Luther, *Treatise on Good Works*, in *Luther's Works*, ed. James Atkinson and Helmut T. Lehmann (Philadelphia: Fortress Press, 1966), 44:23–27, 30, 40, 60.

Bainton, *Here I Stand*, 40–44, 261.

Martin Luther, "Letter to Hans Luther," in *Martin Luther's Basic Theological Writings*, 2nd ed., ed. Timothy F. Lull (Minneapolis: Fortress Press, 2005), 4.

Althaus, *Theology of Martin Luther*, 130–31.

The quotation of Luther's sermon against extrabiblical traditions borrows from two English translations: *Sermons of Martin Luther*, ed. John Nicholas Lenker, vol. 6, *Sermons on Epistle Texts for Advent and Christmas* (Grand Rapids: Baker, 1988), 185; and *What Luther Says*, ed. Ewald M. Plass (St. Louis: Concordia, 1959), 1:85.

Luther, *What Luther Says*, 3:1500–1 and 1512.

Chapter 19: Call

Robertson McQuilken, *A Promise Kept* (Carol Stream, IL: Tyndale, 1998). Online posts include: http://www.christianitytoday.com/ct/2004

/februaryweb-only/2-9-11.0.html; http://www.christianitytoday.com /ct/2004/februaryweb-only/2-9-12.0.html; http://www.familylife.com /articles/topics/marriage/staying-married/commitment/till-death -do-us-part#.ULTOloXaghE; http://www.epm.org/blog/2011/Sep/16 /robertson-mcquilkin-and-joni-eareckson-tada.

Buechner, *Wishful Thinking,* 95.

Gerald Manley Hopkins, "The Principle or Foundation," in *Gerald Manley Hopkins: The Major Works,* ed. Catherine Phillips (New York: Oxford University Press, 2002), 292.

Chapter 20: Fruit

Luther, *Treatise on Good Works,* 23.

Martin Luther, "The Freedom of a Christian," in *Martin Luther's Basic Theological Writings,* 2nd ed., ed. Timothy F. Lull (Minneapolis: Fortress Press, 2005), 404–8.

Jonathan Edwards, *The Religious Affections* (1746; repr., Carlisle, PA: Banner of Truth Trust, 1997), 24, 28, 332.

Chapter 21: Assurance

John Bunyan, *The Pilgrim's Progress,* ed. N. H. Keeble (New York: Oxford University Press, 1998), 8–14.

John Bunyan, *Grace Abounding to the Chief of Sinners,* ed. W. R. Owens (New York: Penguin, 1987), 17, 19, 24, 28, 35–38, 43, 46–47, 73.

Calvin, *Institutes* 3.24.3–4, pp. 968–69.

VanGemeren, Willem A., ed., *New International Dictionary of Old Testament Theology and Exegesis* (Grand Rapids: Zondervan, 1997), 3:1007.

Zachary Ursinus, *The Commentary of Dr. Zacharius Ursinus on the Heidelberg Catechism,* trans. G. W. Williard (Grand Rapids: Eerdmans, 1956), 19–20.

Luther, *What Luther Says,* 1:403.

Martin Luther, "Lectures on Galatians," in *Luther's Works,* ed. James Atkinson and Helmut T. Lehmann (Philadelphia: Fortress Press, 1966), 26:36–37.

Chapter 22: Heroes

Martin Luther, "The Bondage of the Will," in *Martin Luther's Basic Theological Writings*, 2nd ed., ed. Timothy F. Lull (Minneapolis: Fortress Press, 2005), 192–93.

Althaus, *Theology of Martin Luther*, 25–34; and Gerhard O. Forde, *On Being a Theologian of the Cross* (Grand Rapids: Eerdmans, 1997).

Chapter 23: Belief

The quotes from Felix Baumgartner can be found at http://www.bbc.co.uk/news/world-europe-19942836 and "10 Questions," *Time* November 5, 2012, 64.

Josh Groban, "Believe," from the movie *The Polar Express*, words and music by Glen Ballard and Alan Silvestri, Warner Bros., 2004.

Kelly James Clark, "Closing Remarks," in *Five Views on Apologetics*, ed. Steven B. Cowan (Grand Rapids: Zondervan, 2000), 373.

John Piper, *Don't Waste Your Life* (Wheaton: Crossway, 2003), 89, 119.

ACKNOWLEDGMENTS

Writing on faith and doubt is a bit like traversing the Fire Swamp in the movie *The Princess Bride*. I didn't realize until I was halfway in that most of the terms were loaded concepts that might explode at any time, and that stamping out one fire was bound to start a few others. And just when I was knee-deep in explaining the meaning of belief, knowledge, doubt, and risk, here came the rodents of unusual size! I understand Princess Buttercup's cry, "We'll never survive." I really appreciate Westley's determined response, "Nonsense. You're only saying that because no one ever has."

I may smell like smoke, but I believe I made it through without being badly singed—in part because I had some expert guides. I am indebted to Miranda Gardner, who not only fixed my literary tic (the fact that you can't find it shows her skill at her craft) but also raised probing questions about content. I also relied on the theological instincts of friends Jonathan Shelley, Brian McLaughlin, James McGoldrick, Bill Johnson, and Steve Surine, who read this manuscript at various stages and offered wise suggestions for improvement.

And I ran every word by my dear wife, Julie, who besides telling me what worked and what didn't also created the space for me to write. A few months ago Landon said that when he grows up he wants to be an author too. Whether he does or not, I take his desire as a sign that you, Julie, have eased the burden of my calling upon our family. You are my gift from the Lord (Proverbs 18:22).

NOTE TO THE READER

The publisher invites you to share your response to the message of this book by writing Discovery House Publishers, P.O. Box 3566, Grand Rapids, MI 49501, U.S.A. For information about other Discovery House books, music, videos, or DVDs, contact us at the same address or call 1-800-653-8333. Find us on the Internet at www.dhp.org or send e-mail to books@dhp.org.

ABOUT THE AUTHOR

An Ohio native (and demoralized fan of Cleveland sports teams), Mike attended seminary in Grand Rapids, where he has been stuck ever since. He isn't complaining, as West Michigan's many churches and miles of fresh water coastline makes for a fine place to raise a family. He and his wife, Julie, have three school aged children, Avery, Landon, and Alayna. Because of them, he has no hobbies.

When Mike isn't ferrying children to small group or gymnastics practice, he can be found teaching theology at Grand Rapids Theological Seminary. He also enjoys writing books, such as this one, that help Christians to treasure and apply the gospel to their lives. You can follow his thoughts on God and culture at mikewittmer.wordpress.com.